Consumerism

Editor: Danielle Lobban

Volume 414

independence
educational publishers

First published by Independence Educational Publishers

The Studio, High Green

Great Shelford

Cambridge CB22 5EG

England

ISBN-13: 978 1 86168 873 6

Printed in Great Britain

Zenith Print Group

Contents

Introduction

Consumerism is Volume 414 in the **issues** series. The aim of the series is to offer current, diverse information about important issues in our world, from a UK perspective.

ABOUT CONSUMERISM

The way we buy products has drastically changed over the past decade. This book explores the ways we can be savvy consumers, from knowing our consumer rights to understanding how companies make us buy their products.

OUR SOURCES

Titles in the **issues** series are designed to function as educational resource books, providing a balanced overview of a specific subject.

The information in our books is comprised of facts, articles and opinions from many different sources, including:

♦ Newspaper reports and opinion pieces

♦ Website factsheets

♦ Magazine and journal articles

♦ Statistics and surveys

♦ Government reports

♦ Literature from special interest groups.

A NOTE ON CRITICAL EVALUATION

Because the information reprinted here is from a number of different sources, readers should bear in mind the origin of the text and whether the source is likely to have a particular bias when presenting information (or when conducting their research). It is hoped that, as you read about the many aspects of the issues explored in this book, you will critically evaluate the information presented.

It is important that you decide whether you are being presented with facts or opinions. Does the writer give a biased or unbiased report? If an opinion is being expressed, do you agree with the writer? Is there potential bias to the 'facts' or statistics behind an article?

ASSIGNMENTS

In the back of this book, you will find a selection of assignments designed to help you engage with the articles you have been reading and to explore your own opinions. Some tasks will take longer than others and there is a mixture of design, writing and research-based activities that you can complete alone or in a group.

FURTHER RESEARCH

At the end of each article we have listed its source and a website that you can visit if you would like to conduct your own research. Please remember to critically evaluate any sources that you consult and consider whether the information you are viewing is accurate and unbiased.

Useful Websites

www.bbk.ac.uk

www.blog.bham.ac.uk/socialsciencesbirmingham

www.byjus.com

www.consumeradvice.scot

www.dailypost.co.uk

www.epigram.org.uk

www.fastfashionnews.co.uk

www.metro.co.uk

www.proactiveinvestors.co.uk

www.rocketlawyer.com

www.sabguthrie.info

www.savethestudent.org

www.telegraph.co.uk

www.theconversation.com

www.theguardian.com

www.thelawsuperstore.co.uk

www.theminimalistvegan.com

www.yougov.co.uk

Consumer Rights

Difference between customer and consumer

Marketing and advertising include many words that can be difficult for common people to understand. Likewise, many people think that the words Customer and Consumer have a similar meaning, but they have a different meaning from the marketer's viewpoint, though they sound similar. There are various situations where we can understand that the customer and consumer can be the same person, but these words altogether have a different meaning.

Every human being on earth is either a consumer or a customer, in some way or the other, and they are commonly misunderstood. However, a consumer is someone who consumes or uses the goods, and the customer is someone who purchases the commodity and makes the payment.

Sometimes, both the customer and consumer are the same individual, when an individual buys good for their personal use. However, they are not similar, therefore, this article will help you understand the difference between the two. All the marketing processes are aimed towards influencing customers' behaviour, which means to influence the customer so that they take desired action expected by marketers.

Another important feature in the discussion between consumer vs customer is that customers can also be businesses that purchase and then resell goods or merchandise. In such concern, they are only customers and not consumers of the goods they buy because they are reselling it to the consumer to ultimately utilise the product. So let's understand in this article what are the points that make the word customer and consumer different from each other.

Who is a customer?

A customer is a person who buys goods and services regularly from the seller and pays for it to satisfy their needs. Many times when a customer who buys a product is also the consumer, but sometimes it's not. For example, when parents purchase a product for their children, the parent is the customer, and the children are the consumer. They can also be known as clients or buyers.

Customers are divided into two categories:

♦ Trade Customer – These are customers who buy the product, add value and resell it. Like a reseller, wholesaler, and distributor, etc.

♦ Final Customer – These are the customers who buy the product to fulfil their own needs or desires.

Further, according to an analysis of the product satisfaction and relationship with the customers, the customers are divided into three kinds –

♦ Present Customer

♦ Former Customer

♦ Potential Customer

Difference between customer and consumer

Customer

Consumer

Definition

Customer is the one who is purchasing the goods.

Consumer is the one who is the end user of any goods or services.

Ability to resell

Customer can purchase the goods and is able to resell.

Consumers are unable to resell any product or service.

Need for purchase

Customers need to purchase a product or service in order to use it.

For a consumer purchasing a product or service is not essential.

Motive of buying

The motive of buying is either for resale or for consumption.

The motive of buying is only for consumption.

Is payment necessary

Must be paid by customer.

May or may not be paid by the consumer.

Target group

Individual or Company.

Individual, family or group.

Who is a consumer?

A consumer is someone who purchases the product for his/her own need and consumes it. A consumer cannot resell the good or service but can consume it to earn his/her livelihood and self-employment. Any person, other than the buyer who buys the product or services, consumes the product by taking his/her permission is categorized as a consumer. In simple word, the end-user of the goods or services is termed as a consumer.

All individuals who engage themselves in the economy is a consumer of the product. For instance, when a person buys goods from a grocery store for their family, you become a customer, as you are only purchasing the commodities. But, when they feed the grocery to other members of the family, they become the consumer.

Types of customers

In business, customers play a vital role. In fact, customers are the actual boss and responsible for a company to make a profit. A few different types of customers are:

- ◆ Loyal Customer – They are less in numbers but increase more profit and sales as they are completely satisfied with the product or service.

- ◆ Discount Customers – They also regular visitors but buy when they are offered discounts or they purchase only low-cost goods.

- ◆ Impulsive Customers – These types of customers are hard to convince, as they don't go for a specific product, but buy whatever they feel is good and fruitful at that particular point of time.

- ◆ Need-Based Customers – These customers buy only those products which they are in need of or habituated with.

- ◆ Wandering Customers – These are the least valuable customers as they themselves don't know what to purchase.

Types of Consumers

- ◆ A service or product producing firm has to recognise different types of consumers when they target them with its product to gain profits. Some of the different types of consumers are:

- ◆ Commercial Consumer – They buy goods in large numbers whether they need the product or not and sometimes associate special needs with their purchase orders.

- ◆ Discretionary Spending Consumers – They have unique buying habits and purchase a lot of clothes and electronic gadgets.

- ◆ Extroverted Consumer – They prefer brands that are unique and become a loyal consumer once they gain that trust as a customer.

- ◆ Inferior Goods Consumer – Consumer having low-income, buys goods having low price.

Why are consumers important?

The importance of consumers in various avenues is presented below:

1. Encourage Demand – They are the main root for the demand of any product. All manufacturers of goods and services produce various things according to the demand in the market.

2. Create Demand for Various Products – Different consumers have several varieties of demand or an individual consumer can also demand various types of goods. These encourage the manufacturer to deliver various products in the market.

3. Increase Demand for Consumer Goods – It creates demand for various consumer goods, like long-lasting, semi-durable and biodegradable goods.

4. Enhance Service Diversification – Consumers not only utilise different types of products but also use diversified services to support the standard of living. Such as educational service and health service, transport and communication service, and banking and insurance service, etc. This will direct the development or improvement of the service sector in the economy.

Consumer rights

When you buy goods or services as a consumer you have certain rights that protect you in the event that there is something wrong. Make sure you understand your rights as a consumer.

By Millie Johnson

Who is covered?

Consumer rights are only given to consumers. A consumer is someone who purchases goods or services for personal use (ie a private individual buying goods/services for their own personal use). These rights do not apply to businesses or individuals who purchase goods or services on behalf of a business.

What is covered?

These rights apply to any goods or services you buy. Goods can be anything tangible such as a t-shirt, a kettle, a car, second-hand items or goods bought online.

Digital content is covered by consumer rights and can include computer games, films, music, ebooks or mobile apps. However, the rules on digital content are slightly different and complex. For more information, read Consumer rights when purchasing digital content.

Consumer rights apply to any services purchased. Services can cover a wide range of things such as haircuts, dry cleaning, fitted kitchens, bathrooms and home repairs and where goods may also be included as part of a service (eg replacement parts and building materials).

It's important to remember that these rights only apply to goods or services bought after 1 October 2015. Anything bought before that date will have slightly different rights and would require further investigation.

Consumer rights when buying goods

Purchased goods require a certain level of product quality and should meet the following standards:

♦ satisfactory quality

♦ as described

♦ fit for purpose

Satisfactory quality

Satisfactory quality is defined as what a 'reasonable' person would be happy with, looking at all the information readily available such as price (if relevant). Therefore, a luxury or handmade product, like bespoke cupboards or a designer jumper, would have a higher standard as to what is considered satisfactory. In contrast, a second-hand item would have a much lower standard.

As described

The goods should match any description that was provided or was available to you. For example, if a jumper was advertised as being red, but it turned out to be blue, then the jumper was not 'as described'.

Fit for purpose

'Fit for purpose' means that the goods should be usable for their intended purpose. For example, if you bought a pair of shoes and the stitching started to undo after a short while they would not be considered 'fit for purpose'.

What happens if the goods don't meet these standards?

If the goods you purchased don't meet the standards mentioned above, then you should make a direct complaint to the retailer or seller who sold you the goods. This is crucial as some retailers may state that you need to make a claim to the manufacturer instead.

As part of your consumer rights, you have a 30-day right to reject faulty goods. This means that you can state that you no longer want the goods, as they are not of satisfactory quality, as described or fit for purpose, and claim a full refund. The time limit starts from the moment you purchase the goods.

Once the 30-day right to reject has lapsed (ie the 30 days have passed), you will not be legally entitled to a full refund but you still have some rights. You have to give the retailer one opportunity to repair or replace the goods. You may still be able to receive a partial refund instead of a repair or replacement, especially if the cost of repair or replacement is disproportionate (ie the cost of repairing is substantially more than the cost of the original product).

If a fault develops after the first 6 months, then the burden is on the customer who needs to prove that the product was faulty at the time of purchase or delivery. This may require an expert opinion or evidence.

What happens if I just change my mind about the goods?

You won't have an automatic right to get a refund if you decide to change your mind about something you've bought. It will be up to the seller or retailer to decide whether to give you a refund. However, many stores offer a 'goodwill gesture' where they will offer a refund if you've decided to change your mind as long as you provide proof of purchase and the item is in a saleable condition (ie unused or with the tags still attached).

What happens if the delivery is late or if my goods never arrive?

If you bought something that is going to be delivered, it's the seller's responsibility to ensure the item is delivered to you. If the seller used a courier, they should chase the courier to check the status of your order.

If your delivery is late, you should check the delivery address you gave the seller and contact them to ask where your order is. If the seller claims they've delivered it or don't know where it is, you can ask for redelivery. You might be able to get a refund in some circumstances.

For redelivery, you can ask the seller to deliver:

♦ by an agreed date

♦ within a reasonable time (usually within 30 days)

Alternatively, you can cancel and ask for your money back if you don't get the item either:

♦ within 30 days of buying it

♦ on the date you agreed with the seller (if it was essential to receive it by then eg for an event)

♦ on the date of the second chance delivery you agreed with the seller

Consumer rights when buying services

When you buy services, you will also have protection if anything goes wrong. A trader performing a service must:

♦ perform the service with reasonable care and skill

♦ provide the service for a reasonable price, where it was not agreed beforehand

♦ perform the service in a reasonable time period, if it was not agreed beforehand

Reasonable care and skill

This means that the service must be performed to the same standard as other professionals or traders who perform the same service. For example, a hairdresser would be compared to the standard of other hairdressers.

Reasonable price and time period

Where the price for the service was not agreed beforehand, the trader must only charge a reasonable price for the service performed. The same applies to the time period for which the trader must perform the service.

For example, if you had hired a builder to complete home improvements, then where the time period was not agreed beforehand, the trader should complete the work within a reasonable time (ie not too long after the service was paid for).

What happens if the service doesn't meet this criteria?

If the service doesn't meet the above standards, then you can ask the trader:

♦ to redo the part of the service that's inadequate, or perform the whole service again at no extra cost within a reasonable time and without causing you significant inconvenience; or

♦ where it's impossible to repeat the service or can't be done within a reasonable time period, you can claim a price reduction. Depending on how severe or how poorly the service was performed, you could receive up to 100% of the cost. If the trader is going to refund you, they must refund you within 14 days of agreeing to a refund.

What happens if I just change my mind about the service?

If you change your mind about a service you've arranged online, over the phone or by mail-order, you get a 14-day cooling-off period. For example, if you've hired a cleaner or gardener or asked a solicitor to sell your house or a plumber to service your boiler. During the 14 days, you can cancel for any reason and get your money back. However, there are some services to which this does not apply. These include:

♦ accommodation (eg a hotel room or a short-term let)

♦ transport of goods (including courier services)

♦ vehicle rental services

♦ catering or leisure activities for specific dates (eg hotel and restaurant bookings, theatre tickets, catering for a wedding or party)

This cooling-off period doesn't apply where you arranged the service at the business' premises. In these cases, if you have already formalised the contract with the seller and you cancel, you're unlikely to get all your money back. However, it is important to check terms and conditions to see what the cancellation clause states. Usually, there would be a cancellation fee, but you may be able to get some of the money back.

What about goods/services I bought outside of the UK?

If you've bought goods from another country within the EU then you should contact the UK European Consumer Centre for help with problems buying goods or services from another EU country.

What should I do if the retailer won't refund my faulty product?

In the first instance, you should try and resolve this informally with the retailer or seller by contacting them and stating your consumer rights. It's also important to act fast as the entitlement to a full refund only lasts for 30 days from when you bought the goods or services or had it delivered.

You should collect and keep any evidence you have such as pictures of the quality of the product, receipts to act as

How to resolve consumer disputes the right way

Your consumer rights protect you when you've bought faulty goods, items that weren't as advertised, or received otherwise poor service. If you're involved in a consumer dispute, you could be entitled to a refund or replacement.

By Steve Clark

proof of purchase, contracts you signed or any terms and conditions available to you.

In any event, provided that you are located in England and Wales, you can make a claim to the Small Claims Court if the retailer or seller is being uncooperative.

If you are located in Scotland, you can make a court claim for money to the Sheriff Court. However, this should always be used as a last resort.

You can also make a complaint to the Consumer Ombudsman or your local Citizens Advice Bureau. The Citizens Advice Bureau have a dedicated Consumer Service helpline and can help you lodge a complaint and enforce your consumer rights.

What happens if a faulty product damages my property?

If a faulty product has caused damage to your property (eg a leaking faulty washing machine causing damage to flooring) then you may be able to claim the costs of rectifying the damage from the retailer or seller.

However, you will only be able to claim compensation for damage if the cost of the damage is more than £275. The total amount that you can claim will depend on the harm suffered, but there is no upper limit to compensation.

The process for making a claim for compensation is the same as the process used to request a refund described above.

Do I have a right to repair?

From 1 July 2021, The Ecodesign for Energy-Related Products and Energy Information Regulations 2021 (the Ecodesign Regulations) introduced rights for consumers granting further rights to repairs to defective home appliances. Under the Ecodesign Regulations, spare parts for certain electric appliances repairs must be made available for repairs without consumers having to show the cause of the defect.

What are my consumer rights?

Your consumer rights are covered by the Consumer Rights Act 2015. Its purpose is to strengthen and clarify your rights as a shopper.

Before being introduced, consumer rights and laws were spread across 10 different parliamentary Acts. Most were written in what the government called 'legalistic language' and none of them made allowances for rapidly changing technology.

The purpose of the Consumer Rights Act is to protect you after receiving shoddy services, goods, or digital content, giving you the right to recompense.

What's covered in a consumer dispute?

Whether it's a used car or a digital download, anything and everything you buy should be:

♦ Fit for purpose

♦ Of satisfactory quality

♦ As described

Deliveries are also covered by your consumer rights. So, if you paid for something that didn't arrive, you're well within your rights to take further action.

It doesn't matter where you bought the goods or services, if a product doesn't meet one or all of these standards, then your rights have been breached.

You have a set time to deal with the problem. The way the law deals with goods, services, and digital content differs slightly.

Consumer disputes over goods bought at home or in a shop

Once you take ownership of your goods, you have 30 days to get a full refund if it's faulty. If purchased in a store, you're entitled to an immediate refund.

If your goods can't be repaired or replaced after 6 months, then you'll likely qualify for a full refund.

Goods should last a fair amount of time – depending on what you've bought, this could be up to 6 years. If they don't, you could get some of your money back.

Consumer disputes over digital content

Digital content like games, apps, movies, and music is governed under the Consumer Contracts Regulations, giving you 14 days to raise the issue with the supplier.

But there's a catch.

When you buy digital content, you're granted the usual 14-day cooling off period – but the moment you download it, you waive your right to this. This stops people seeking refunds right after purchase.

There's often a grey area between buying digital content and downloading it.

If you purchase a pre-paid download code but don't input it, you're still entitled to your 14-day cooling off period.

In most cases, though, the act of buying it leads to a download – for example, purchasing an eBook that's automatically downloaded to your tablet or a video game that instantly installs on your computer.

When that happens, the provider's terms of services will state that when buying the content, you're waiving your rights to the cooling off period.

At that point, you can get a repair or replacement if the digital content is faulty.

If the fault can't be fixed, you can get a full or partial refund.

And if the digital content broke another device – like crashing your computer – the company may have to repair it or provide compensation.

Services paid for in a shop or ordered at home

Services covers everything from restaurants to building work. The Consumer Rights Act 2015 makes it clear that any service must be performed with reasonable care and skill, at a reasonable price, delivered within a reasonable time.

You can cancel within 14 days of purchase to get a refund.

If a service fails the 'reasonable time and skill' test, you can ask for the service to be repeated or fixed. If it can't be, you can get a partial refund.

Who can help when my consumer rights have been affected?

Taking a consumer complaint to the courts should be the last resort – the law expects you to have tried solving the issue before the dispute reaches them.

Contact the seller first

When you're involved in a consumer dispute, your first step is to contact the seller. Take that broken microwave back to the shop you bought it from (and make sure you pack proof of purchase); call the national helpline over that poor tyre-fitting.

If this yields no results, or you didn't buy it in-store, make a complaint in writing. Outline the issue in your complaint, how it breaches your statutory rights, and explain how you'd like it to be resolved. Send letters via recorded delivery, for extra insurance.

In most cases, the company will want to sort this out as quickly as possible with a replacement or refund. You may be asked to return the faulty product if ordered online or through a catalogue – and, if you haven't had the product long, you're entitled to a refund on shipping costs here.

Contact an ombudsman and Trading Standards

If the company or seller doesn't respond to your complaint, or you choose to reject their solution, it's worth checking if you can lodge a report with an ombudsman or Trading Standards.

An ombudsman is an independent, impartial adjudicator that oversees complaints in their specific sector, e.g., banking or law. Use the Ombudsman Association to see if there's one for you.

Trading Standards is the organisation that investigates complaints about dodgy business practices or selling illegal goods and services.

How can I resolve a consumer dispute through court action?

If you're just not getting any joy, it's time to consider taking the seller to court. This is a big step, so it's worth discussing your claim with a consumer disputes solicitor.

If you want to claim up to £10,000

Claims under £10,000 are considered small claims.

Before making your claim online, you should send another letter or email to the seller letting them know you intend to take the matter further.

This letter must also detail your name, address, the complaint, how much you believe is owed, and the expected resolution (even if you've already sent a letter saying much the same). Give them a deadline to respond – usually, 14 days.

The government's online claim form should only be used when requesting a specific amount of money. Other claims, typically for services, should be made by printing and posting the N1 form.

When making a small claim, you'll also need to pay a fee, which ranges from £25 for claims up to £300, right up to £410 to claim up to £10,000.

If you want to claim between £10,001 and £100,000

Claims that exceed the 'small claims court' threshold should be discussed with a solicitor.

Use the Money Claim Online, administered by HM Courts & Tribunals Service. This can be completed either by you or your solicitor. You may also be entitled to interest on the money owed, too.

12 May 2022

How to complain successfully

Dodgy shoes? Cold soup? Bad phone signal? These are all very valid reasons to complain, and you should always speak out if something's not up to scratch.

By Jem Collins

When you've parted with your hard-earned cash for something, you're well within your rights to expect your money back if the service or goods aren't up to scratch.

But, it's often hard to get past the worry that you won't be taken seriously if you try to complain.

Ultimately, knowing how and when to complain is crucial. To help, we've put together a comprehensive guide to complaining successfully. Feel free to complain if it's not good enough.

How to make a complaint

Here is how to make a complaint and get results:

Decide if your complaint is justified

This might sound obvious, but picking the right time to raise an issue is just as important as actually making the complaint.

Whatever you're thinking of complaining about, don't do it if you're only looking to get free stuff out of it.

Not only will it be painfully obvious that this is your intention if that's all you're gunning for, but it could lead to you being banned from somewhere as a result if you're busted.

Valid reasons to make a complaint

- ♦ You received a service (such as a massage or a haircut) that was inadequate

- ♦ Staff were rude or made you feel uncomfortable (e.g. in a restaurant or shop)

- ♦ You were served something very substandard or that didn't meet an expected level of health and safety (like if you find a hair in your meal)

- ♦ A product you bought was faulty or didn't work as it should

- ♦ A service or goods were delivered unreasonably late

- ♦ You were overcharged for something

- ♦ You were unable to return an item, even though you complied with the store's return policy

- ♦ A company hasn't satisfied all of its contractual obligations (e.g. you were promised 500 free minutes and unlimited texts, but only got the calls).

Consider what you want to achieve from the complaint

It's all very well knowing that the hot dog you ordered was delivered by a grumpy sod that made you feel about as wanted as a steak in a vegetarian restaurant, but you need to give the company some idea of what it would take to get back in your good books.

The three main methods of fixing customer complaints are:

- ♦ Offering you an exchange or fixing the problem

- ♦ Refunding you for the goods or service

- ♦ Offering compensation.

While you may not be automatically entitled to compensation or a refund in every circumstance, it's more likely to be achievable if you know what you're looking for.

Have a think about exactly what you want to be offered in response to your complaint before you make it, and it'll make the process a lot easier.

Research your consumer rights

Before you go in all guns blazing, make sure you've got all the facts first.

Write down a full description of the issue and research what your rights are. Try consulting our guide to your consumer rights and have a quick search on Google for advice on your particular situation.

Any photos, receipts or comments from witnesses that you can gather can help with your case – the more info and material you have when you make the complaint, the better chance you'll have of resolving the issue effectively.

If the complaint's about a purchase, try to state the exact time that you were in the store or making the order, too. This sort of info (combined with a description of the staff member who served you) can hugely help a company to decide whether further action needs to be taken.

The added bonus of this stage is that gathering all the info and writing it down can be kind of cathartic. Once you've blown off some steam doing this, you might even find it a bit easier to lodge your complaint without losing your rag.

Stay calm when making a complaint

We understand that you won't be at your happiest after a disappointing incident or purchase. However, remember that the people you're dealing with are human too, and they're just trying to do their job.

What's more, those involved will be much more inclined to help you out if you treat them with respect – even if you are absolutely fuming inside. After all, it's highly unlikely that they were directly responsible for the problem in the first place.

If you're calm and collected, you're also much more likely to explain your situation coherently and with enough detail for the issue to be resolved successfully.

Complain as quickly as possible

You should always complain as soon as possible after the event to stand the best chance of getting a positive end result. This is especially true if you're complaining about

Writing a formal complaint

Putting your complaint in writing is a good shout if you can't physically go there – that way you've got solid proof of all communication. This could be via letter (if you're old school) or email, addressed to the relevant person.

If the company does decide to send you some free things or money in the post, the whole process will be much easier if you include your full details in your complaint. This will be covered if you're writing a formal complaint letter, as your address should be written at the top.

Make sure to include any statutory rights you feel have been broken in your letter, and ask the company (politely) to get back to you within a reasonable time frame so you're not left hanging. This also makes it much easier to chase up if they don't stick to the date.

faulty goods – and make sure you stop using them as soon as you notice there's an issue.

After all, would you really believe someone was distraught about the service they received in store if they only got round to complaining six weeks later? Or that a frying pan was totally unfit for purpose from day one, but it's obvious that they carried on using it for a fortnight?

If there's a reason you haven't been able to complain earlier, be sure to clarify this in your complaint.

Follow a company's complaints procedure

At this stage, going straight to the manager or owner of the company to tell them their business is shambolic might feel tempting, but you can often sort out complaints much faster if you start at the source of the issue.

If your problem involves something that happened in a place where you were present or with something you bought in-store, you should first ask to speak to the person who (in your eyes) caused the problem in the first place.

In many cases, they'll be happy to solve the issue there and then as the last thing they'll want is for the complaint to go further up to a manager.

Alternatively, if your complaint is about a product and the store has a customer services department, it's worth going straight there first – it's their job to keep you happy!

If your issue involves something you bought online, then the first port of call should be to check the company's website or social media for a customer service email.

Complain in person or write a formal letter

If your complaint is about an item you bought from a shop, get yourself down there in person rather than doing it over the phone. It's far harder for someone to ignore or overlook your complaint if you're making it face-to-face.

If there's absolutely no other way for you to contact them than over the phone, keep a full record of the conversation by jotting down the most important points and make sure you get the name of the person you're dealing with.

Lastly, check your spelling. Bad spelling doesn't excuse a company for not dealing with your complaint properly, but it will help give a good impression and show you're serious about your issue if you've proofread your complaint before sending it.

Make a complaint on social media

If you're a confident writer and feel like you have a strong case, you might even want to try your hand at writing a viral complaint or making a complaint video that could gain thousands of views.

No business likes to receive complaint tweets for all to see (although everyone gets them), so they're more likely to want to be seen to offer a solution ASAP to protect their image.

If your matter is too elaborate for 280 characters, or it's a more personal matter, simply send them a direct message about your complaint.

Still no reply? Badger them on all their social media channels until you get a response (but don't use aggressive language!), and if you're still having no luck, send a formal letter to the company's head office. Which brings us to our next point...

Contact the company's head office

You can attempt to contact someone very high up by searching for their email address on this website. Alternatively, you can try to guess (e.g. alansmith@company.co.uk, asmith@company.co.uk or a.smith@company.co.uk etc.).

You may notice a profile picture pop up next to an email address when you type it in – this shows you are using a valid email address and is (hopefully!) the intended recipient.

The higher up you take your complaint, the more people you'll end up speaking to. It's always useful to be able to reference how you've tried to resolve the problem already, as this shows how seriously you're taking the complaint and avoids any 'he said, she said' situations.

What to do if your complaint is ignored or dismissed

If your complaint is ignored or dismissed, you can do the following:

Go to an ombudsman

An ombudsman is a form of ADR scheme (Alternative Dispute Resolution scheme) which you can reach out to if you've exhausted all other options and are still not getting anywhere.

The ombudsman will only act if an admin or service error has occurred, so you can't go to them if your complaint is more about a difference of opinion (bad customer service, for example).

Major UK ombudsman services

♦ Ofgem is a government-run regulator that deals with issues between you and your energy provider, for both gas and electricity.

♦ The Financial Ombudsman Service resolves disputes between financial services such as banks, insurers and lenders, and their customers. They'll give you an unbiased opinion and have the legal powers to correct any wrongdoing.

♦ Ofcom deal with complaints regarding communication services like your phone contract or broadband provider.

♦ The Competition and Markets Authority deal with issues of competition in business, and as part of their work, they make sure universities comply with consumer law. If you're thinking about filing a complaint against your university, you may want to get in touch with them.

These are some of the leading ombudsman services, but there are different types of ADRs for different sectors. For complaints in other areas, a quick Google should bring up the relevant contact.

Take your complaint to a small claims court

If your complaint involves a breach of contract, you can try to take it to a small claims court. The maximum amount you can claim for with small claims is £10,000 in England and Wales, £5,000 in Scotland and £3,000 in Northern Ireland.

Speak to Citizens Advice

Finally, if you're really struggling to get anywhere with the company, then you might want to look into taking legal action – depending on how serious the claim is.

If you've exhausted all the options available within the company itself and still aren't happy, there are people you can go to for help.

The Citizens Advice Bureau offer free advice to anyone on money, legal or other issues and you can either call, email or pop into a local centre to chat with them.

5 April 2022

UK customer service complaints reach record high

The Institute of Customer Service found that UK firms are spending over £9 billion every month to cover complaints handling.

By Jai Singh

Customer service complaints have hit their highest level on record, new research has found.

The Institute of Customer Service (ICS) found that the number of consumers experiencing service issues was the highest since its UK Customer Satisfaction Index began in 2008.

The ICS survey, which polled 10,000 consumers across 13 industries, found that UK firms are spending a total of £9.24 billion every month to cover complaints handling.

According to the data, shortages and supply chain issues have led to a 16% rise in customer problems, typically over quality and reliability of goods and services.

It showed 17.3% of UK customers are experiencing a product or service problem – the highest level since it launched in 2008.

The best rated company for handling complaints in ICS's customer satisfaction index was infrastructure provider UK Power Networks, after strong communication and compensation payouts following storms Eunice and Franklin earlier this year.

Timpson, John Lewis Tesco Mobile, Suzuki and Marks & Spencer all also improved their scores from the last survey.

Specsavers was the biggest faller out of the top 50 companies, dropping 38 places from ninth in 47 since the last survey in July 2021.

5 July 2022

I'd like to make a complaint... Why some of us are so good at making a fuss

Were you the child whose indignant letter yielded a free bar of chocolate? Séamas O'Reilly puts pen to paper to reveal why we are a nation of complainers.

By Séamas O'Reilly

The biscuit was only barely covered. If I'd had to guess, I'd have said 30% of its surface had chocolate applied, and that's being charitable. Certainly more charitable than the manufacturer of the Jaffa Cake in question, who I pictured as God's perfect miser; a Scrooge-like figure toiling in a candle-lit factory, peering over their bifocals to smear homeopathic levels of chocolate on one sorry corner of my favourite tea snack. I was 10 years old, and had never had a particularly strong sense of myself as a consumer champion, but this biscuit, this disgrace, roused something inside me.

'Dear McVitie's,' I wrote, addressing the entire company in my missive. 'I was shocked and appalled to discover this Jaffa Cake (enclosed) in such a state.' In hindsight, I was savvy enough to moderate my speech to sound adult, but not perhaps worldly enough to consider enclosing the foodstuff itself in plastic before popping it in with my letter. By the time I posted it the following day, I remember already noticing some of its soft greasiness had permeated the envelope, but I reckoned this was probably just the way things were done. Evidently it was, as two weeks later I received a letter apologising for my suboptimal experience, along with an invitation to tour a factory, and two whole boxes of Jaffa Cakes. These, I am happy to report, were perfectly chocolated.

That victory won, I retired from professional complaining, preserving my 100% record in amber for all time. Others, however, have kept the faith. The 18th century's finest polymath, Samuel Johnson, once said: 'Man alone is born crying, lives complaining and dies disappointed.' It would seem that the British public has taken this more as a recommendation than a rebuke. While canvassing people for this article, I received more than 150 replies in 24 hours and read, amazed, as a grateful public unloaded stories of consumer activism, tweet by tweet.

In 2019, the Mirror reported that 33% of UK residents polled had left a negative review online, and 70% of those had done so within the past year. Two weeks later, the Daily Mail lamented the findings of an entirely different study claiming Brits spend 10,000 minutes of their year complaining (a moral high ground it would have been easier to maintain had they not embedded that very article with links to their own columnists complaining about woke millennials). Perhaps 'mentor7' summed up the mood of that room best in the comment he left under that article, saying: 'It's wonderful. There's so much to moan about every day and it's on the increase. I love moaning. It makes me so happy.'

> '**Dear McVitie's, I wrote, I was shocked and appalled to discover this Jaffa Cake (enclosed) in such a state**'

This outlook may now be the rule rather than the exception. Ofcom's recent report for the 2020-21 financial year revealed it had received more than 145,000 complaints about broadcasts, a 400% increase on last year's figure of 34,545. (Additional to those numbers, the BBC received 110,000 complaints about the wall-to-wall coverage of Prince Philip's death alone.) So what has caused this boom in belly-aching?

'The numbers can be explained by a few big-ticket items,' says Adam Baxter, director of broadcast standards at Ofcom. 'Just before the end of that reporting period, this March, there was the issue around Piers Morgan and his comments about the Duchess of Sussex. That got north of 50,000 complaints by itself. Last September, we also had the Diversity dance troupe's performance on Britain's Got Talent [which included imagery and messaging in support of the Black Lives Matter movement] and we got over 24,000 complaints for that. Those two incidents alone accounted for more than half the complaints. But, even if you discounted those, you're still looking at 70,000+ complaints, which is a huge increase in and of itself.'

Baxter is open-hearted and expressive in conversation, very much the kind of person to whom you'd be delighted to complain about a faulty Jaffa Cake. At one point during our video interview, the connection stalls. Cursed by comedic genius, I ask if I can make a complaint about my broadband service through him. He politely tells me that would fall under telecoms not broadcast, but in a tone that suggests he'd probably pass me to the right person if I wanted. He certainly doesn't see the recent rise in complaints and complainers as signs of a nationwide tendency for tedious begrudgery, and rather views it as a natural expression of public interest.

'I really love my job,' he says, 'when people find out I work for Ofcom, they will always have opinions about what they've seen and watched on telly or heard on radio – often very strong opinions. If they know something has had loads of complaints they'll always ask me what I think. Of course, I have to be careful and very politely say, 'Oh, how interesting,' without saying whether I think it's right or wrong.'

The breadth of Ofcom's remit is fairly staggering. Baxter oversees a team of 40, within Ofcom's 1,000-strong staff, charged with the thankless task of assessing every complaint that comes in related to breaches of the broadcast code. In practice, this is exactly as large a job as it sounds, involving a mammoth amount of data capture and analysis.

'We have a wonderful bit of software that grabs all the most prominent channels for complaints. So, if we get a complaint, we can go to that bit of the software and pull the recording. If we don't record a channel in-house, we will write to the broadcaster and they have five working days to come back to us with a recording.' This extends to the process of assessing non-English-language programming with dedicated staff trained for precisely this purpose. 'We have in-house translators for some of the languages that have recurring complaints about incitement to religious hatred and hate speech. I have a team fluent in Urdu, Punjabi, Pashtu and Arabic, and they'll often be doing the recording'.

For a view from the ground floor, I spoke with former complaints desk operator, 'Paul', who spent years working on the phones, answering queries that came in from members of the public across all of Ofcom's remit.

'When I was there,' he says, 'the type of people who complained about broadband or their phone company would be ordinary people who've had a bad experience, who were complaining because something was costing them money or was a major inconvenience. But when I was getting calls through the broadcast queue' – he pauses – 'I was almost expecting them to be a little eccentric. I already had my guard up.'

He recalls one example, from more than a decade ago, like it was yesterday. 'I remember speaking to some guy for 20 minutes because he was upset about a repeat of Trisha that featured a phone-in. Because it was a repeat, text on the screen said: 'Lines are now closed – this is a repeat.' This guy was incensed. I said: 'You didn't call in, did you?' And he said, 'No, but it's not very nice is it?' I told him their only other choice would be not to run repeats…'

Paul's attempts at conciliation fell on deaf ears. Then he realised his caller was not upset by false advertising, but that it contradicted his favourite TV presenter. 'They're making Trisha out to be a right mug: she's saying phone in and as she's doing that, on the screen it says, 'Don't bother.' They're making her look stupid.'

Paul had previously worked at the Advertising Standards Authority, which gave him a further insight into the machinations of the Great British Complainer. 'When I was there,' he recalls, 'the most complained-about ad had nothing to do with racism, sexism, or misleading or fraudulent content' but a KFC ad that enraged viewers because it featured office workers singing with their mouths full of chicken salad. He pauses for emphasis. 'It wasn't just like that one crept over the line and beat the record, it completely smashed the record. People went apeshit over that ad.'

To some extent, the pull of complaining may be tied to this need to get something off one's chest, or to strike back against corporate or media behemoths that seem untouchable to the lesser mortals who use their services. Software designer Barney Carroll intuits a deeper, sociological reasoning for our need to complain. 'Jovially indignant stories about complaining to customer services until you got loads of cool stuff,' he says, 'seemed to me an intrinsic component of my grandparents' experience of the postwar social contract.'

Or maybe we're all just children, pretending to be adults, in order to secure free chocolate. Musician Emma Langford was one of many people I spoke with who assured me my Jaffa Cake activism was in no way unique.

'As a kid I got a box of Milk Tray and the Turkish delights were solid chocolate,' she told me. 'I wrote a distraught letter of complaint but – assuming I wouldn't be taken seriously as a kid – I posed as an adult man who bought them for his wife'. Furnishing me with a photo of the letter, now tattered from its position as a well-worn family heirloom, it was clear her story checked out.

'To whom it may concern,' it begins, in the time-honoured manner of every child hoping to sound like an adult. 'I am writing in complaint of one of your boxes of chocolates.' However, the letter's fussy tone reaches its peak in the following paragraph. 'On The 10th of February, I purchased a box of your confectionary selections, Cadbury's Milk Tray, for Valentine's Day as a romantic gesture towards my wife.'

If the mechanisms by which we complain have changed, the central urge may be the same as it's always been, only now enabled by the instant gratification of social media and dedicated teams of people combing through our concerns about broadcasts, faulty biscuits and the horror of people singing with their mouths full. There is also the possibility that a year indoors has sharpened our sense of irritability, while keeping us free of the distractions that blighted the careers of previous generations of complainers, stifling their ability to complain as freely as we can now. Perhaps it's not surprising that Covid coverage has itself been cited in 14,000 complaints to Ofcom in the past year.

'We've no detailed deep-dive on the reasons people complain,' concludes Baxter, who is resolutely thoughtful and empathetic when discussing complainers. 'Clearly,' he says, 'it's a range of things. It captures the gamut of human emotions. There are people who are very agitated and angry, especially depending on the issue, and people who just want to vent rather than address that issue, per se. There is some anecdotal feedback of people writing back to us – not many, to be brutally frank – whose complaints haven't been upheld, and saying: 'I don't agree with your decision, but thanks for taking the time to explain it to me.' Perhaps, then, his isn't such a thankless task after all.

12 June 2021

'Doing it for the kids' – the impact of consumerism on teenagers and young adults

By Colin Mathieson

As an adult, I cringe when I think about the (questionable) decisions made in my youth to dress in baggy jeans, with stainless steel chains looped from belt to pocket. My hair was black with an 'electric-blue' tint and I could often be found clad in a hooded sweatshirt with my favourite band plastered on the front. My friends all dressed almost identically. Rather ironically, we believed that our 'individual' or 'alternative' style defined who we were and made us stand out from the crowd.

Unsurprisingly, this was not the case. Our usual Saturday day out was spent standing with another thirty to forty people who were dressed identically to us, listening to the same music and making the same sweeping statements about their own individuality and their unique perspective on the world.

The irony here is that this is not a standalone phenomenon specific to my generation. 'Fitting in', whilst having the courage to demonstrate one's own individuality is an important part of growing up. Referred to as one of our most 'creative and controlled behaviours', consumer consumption is widely acknowledged as an activity which allows individuals to do exactly this. Living within a consumer-focused society can offer people the creative licence to demonstrate a certain level of self-awareness and self-expression.

However, there are obvious negatives associated with such a choice. With the rise of social media, product placement and targeted advertising, we are continually bombarded with images of products and services which promise to make our lives easier, more glamorous and essentially better than those around us. This inevitably raises concerns regarding the impact of this exposure on the more easily influenced or vulnerable members of our society. Young people are often the worst affected, forced to keep up with the latest trends in order to feel fulfilled and/or accepted by their peers.

The highly regarded sociologist, Zygmunt Bauman, separated consumers into two camps, those he referred to as the 'seduced' and the 'repressed'. This sought to highlight the basic level of inequality which consumerism can cause. Consumer choice is only truly available to those who have the necessary financial resources. This is necessary to afford the latest trends, such as the newest branded trainers or the latest version of a mobile phone.

The 'repressed' are those individuals forced to stand on the periphery, forced into situations where they compete with peers to keep up with the latest trends. This can force many to resort to cheaper alternatives, such as counterfeit goods, copy-cat brands (where they get the bargain but not the same shelf-life). We have previously written about the impacts that counterfeit goods have on consumers and the economy.

All these factors lead us to question whether we always exert personal choice as consumers or are our consumer choices ultimately controlled? Are we pushed and pulled in certain directions by retailers vying for our money? In order to fully understand the spending practices of teenagers and young adults, it is necessary to assess where society at large is 'pulled' or 'pushed' into making consumer decisions, regardless of the scale.

6 December 2019

How to avoid the trap of consumerism

By Michael Ofei

What is consumerism? According to Wikipedia, consumerism is a social and economic order that encourages the acquisition of goods and services in ever-increasing amounts.

The definition sounds reasonable until the last couple of words, 'ever-increasing amounts.'

Consumerism implies that we exponentially acquire goods even if that means going into debt, compromising health or wasting precious time while we're still alive.

How do we avoid consumerism in a world that's engineered to make us endlessly desire more? Well, we can't.

I know that's a bit of a downer answer, but it's the truth, my friends. We must fundamentally consume to survive.

While we can't 100% reject consumerism, we do have the power to avoid the limitless vortex of excessiveness and get some agency over our lives.

In this article, we explore 13 strategies to help you curb your consumption habits. They'll be some things you're already aware of (and need a friendly reminder), but there are also a bunch of unique suggestions in here, which I'm excited to share with you!

However, before we get into the juicy tips, we need to see if you're suffering from the symptoms of excessive consumerism.

The symptoms of excessive consumerism

So you think you've got your consumerism under control? Below are 9 signs that you still have some work to do.

1. You buy more than you planned: if you set out with a plan of what you need to purchase but consistently come back with more than you anticipated, then you're falling in the consumerist trap.

2. You run out of storage space for your stuff: sometimes it can't be helped if you live in a tight area or you're disorganised. But suppose you're in a reasonable situation and things you bring in don't have an allocated home. In that case, you're likely living excessively.

3. You rely too much on return policies: returning an item is useful. Particularly if you need to test a product for the intended purpose, be it sizing for clothes or a tool for a building project. However, suppose you're depending on returns for purchases. In that instance, you're not sure you need it, or if you can't afford it, then you're probably suffering from too much consumerism.

4. You routinely seek approval for your purchases: getting feedback on purchases can be reassuring, especially if you're indecisive. Yet, there's a difference between picking someone's brain before buying and looking to justify your purchase after the fact. If you're seeking post-acquisition approval, you probably don't need the item.

5. You mistakenly buy things you already have: not much to say here. If you're getting things only to realise you already have it, then you're probably deep in a consumerist cycle.

6. You buy things on credit: if you're strategic and disciplined, you can buy things on credit cards to acquire points and benefits. However, if you're like the majority of us, then you're vulnerable to buying things you can't afford.

7. You constantly go over your budget: sometimes, you miss-forecast how much you need to spend each month. But if you set a realistic budget and find that you're still going over, then you're probably consuming excessively.

8. You regret your purchases: the most obvious sign that you have a shopping habit is you regret things you bought. Buyer's remorse is an overwhelming feeling and one we want to avoid.

9. You're hiding purchases: when I was 19, I took out a loan to buy a brand new motorcycle. I hid it in my neighbours' garage because I was scared and embarrassed to show my parents. Did I need the bike? Nope. Could I afford the motorcycle? Nope. Was I an excessive consumer? You bet! If you're hiding purchases from your loved ones, you undoubtedly have some consumerism issues.

How did you go? Do you have any of the above symptoms? If not, kudos to you!

13 strategies to reduce consumerism

Here's a breakdown of actions you can start implementing today.

1. Replace fast purchasing with slow purchasing

When we start losing control of our consumption habits, it's usually because we're making quick, impulsive decisions.

We reactively say yes to things we haven't fully thought through and instead consume with our emotions.

Emotions should fuel our decisions, but our minds should be driving the car to ensure everyone makes it to the destination safely.

One way to make sure that your mind is in the driver's seat is to slow down your buying process. The simplest way to do this is to write down a list of the things you need or want, then take the time to research the best option. Give the process space instead of acting hastily.

If you need to buy something urgently, first reflect on why you're in an urgent situation. Is it because an event randomly came up that you couldn't control, and you need to act swiftly? Or is it a result of your lack of planning?

If you need to make a quicker decision, still take a moment to slow it down.

For example, instead of going straight to the shops to buy an item that needs urgent replacing, research the options online, first reading reviews and watching a video or two. Even call ahead to your local outlets to see if they have the good in stock.

Another benefit to slow purchasing is you have more time to find a second-hand option or even borrow the item if it's a temporary need. More on that later.

By slowing down your purchasing process, you're giving the power to your mind over your emotions. You move from a reactive state of consumption to a focused and proactive mindset. When you make this shift, you reduce the chance of acquiring something you don't need or won't use.

2. Make the buying process inconvenient

I recognise for many of us, shopping is like a fun game. The system of consumerism is designed to be addictive, which is all part of the trap.

In the New York Times best-selling book Atomic Habits, author James Clear talks about how the best way to stop bad habits is to make them inconvenient and unattractive.

So if we want to ease up on our shopping habits, how can we make the process difficult?

One approach that's worked incredibly well for me is to adopt a mindful consumer mindset. What this means is acquiring items that not only perform well but are also ethical and eco-friendly.

By layering on these requirements to what you consume, you instantly shrink your options. It makes the process of shopping more tedious as a result.

Do you know how hard it is to go down to your local retail department store and find clothing made from organic materials? Most of the time, the shop assistants won't be able to give you any clarity on the supply chain of the brands they stock.

When you realise it will be challenging to find a sustainable version of what you want, you automatically slow down your purchasing process. This makes the experience of shopping a little more off-putting.

Other examples of making consumerism inconvenient include:

- Deleting any app on your phone or tablet that's related to buying stuff. Yes, that includes your internet browsers.

- Moving to a remote area where you're forced to plan your trips into town, and you generally have poorer access to the internet. This is an extreme example but effective nevertheless.

- Cut up your credit cards and remove them from your devices. If you remember your card number, order a replacement card before destroying it.

3. Pass the mall test

I grew up in a city with a mall (or shopping centres as we call them in Australia) in every region.

The mall was the place to hang out with my buddies, eat in the food court, and, of course, buy stuff I didn't need.

I remember deciding to buy a Nintendo with a mate after a 20-minute conversation or buying a jacket for a 'buy one get one free' deal within minutes of seeing it.

I realise malls don't have the same allure as they used to, but they're still a consumerist hub for many of us.

As I've stepped into minimalism, the mall represents an entirely different experience to me.

When I enter a shopping centre today, it feels chaotic, overwhelming, confusing and sad.

The conventional advice to reduce consumerism is to avoid going to the mall altogether. I think this is a positive start. However, it's even better if you can go to the mall and not become susceptible to all the stimulation.

So here's the exercise. Next time you go to the mall, think of yourself as a researcher (not a browser), take a step back, and do some people-watching.

Observe what people are contemplating buying. Listen in to their conversations (without stalking). Spend at least an hour strolling through the mall as you do your observations. It's actually fascinating!

A pattern I've observed is the variety of justifications we make when considering a purchase. The conversations people have with shop assistants and/or their spouses are no different to the conversations you have in the same situations.

You'll hear comments like:

'How long is the sale for?'

'I do need to replace x?'

'What do you think?'

'What's your return policy?'

'Mummy, can I get this?'

These are the statements I've picked up, but your experience may be different.

In any case, by observing people, you start to see the mall in a completely different light. You understand the truth of the framework and how we play a role in the system.

I still believe we can enjoy the mall (if you choose to) and do some window shopping, chat with shop assistants or friends you randomly bump into. You could play some games at the arcade without cashing out your tickets on stuffed toys.

Use the mall as a measuring stick of your self-control. Do you think you can pass the test?

4. Declutter to discover the truth

You know when you're moving house, and you're downright horrified by how many things you have?

I experienced this a few years ago. It looked like we didn't have much on the surface, but things kept flowing out of our storage spaces to show us the truth.

The amount of clutter you have is a reflection of your consumption habits.

This is the equivalent of checking your bank balance before making a financial plan. Or taking your body measurements before working towards a health transformation.

So instead of waiting to move houses, take the time to declutter your environment. Decluttering will reveal your behaviours and give you some extra motivation to become better at managing your consumeristic tendencies.

5. Extend the lifespan of your things

Repairing your things is not only an effective way to reduce your consumption, but it's also beneficial to the environment.

Suppose you have the skills to knit your sweater or reinstate your coffee table. In that case, you're probably already utilising your talents. But if you're like me and don't possess any special trade skills, you can seek support from your community.

Do you have a handy friend or relative? Do you have a repair cafe in your area?

Alternatively, you could pay for the services of a shoe smith or take your iPhone into the Genius Bar.

By extending the lifecycle of your things, it gives you a greater respect for everything you possess. Naturally, you become more intentional about what you bring into your life.

6. Reframe shopping as a skill

Sometimes we can take on the identity of being a crafty shopper who can find quality things at a bargain price.

We brag to our friends prompting them to guess how much we paid for a particular item.

The more we reinforce a shopper's identity, the more time we want to spend improving the skill – thus consuming excessively.

If we're not careful, we end up shopping for the sake of shopping, while failing to realise why we were shopping in the first place.

Try reframing shopping from an event to a mission of finding the most appropriate tool that will help you have the best experience.

For example, after being car-less for a year, my wife and I bought a 1999 Toyota Tarago despite not having any dependents.

The Tarago (which we named Maurie) was our getaway vehicle. We bought this car because it was cheap and intended to put all of the things we owned into the van as we moved states. Maurie represented change and adventure.

There was never a focus on the process of buying the vehicle. Maurie was merely playing a role in a greater experience.

When you focus on the role the thing you're buying will play in the overall experience instead of the experience of shopping itself, you'll be able to shift away from a consumerist mindset.

7. Avoid the trap of 'free'

You receive a secret Santa gift at work.

A friend offers you their rice cooker.

The local real estate agent gives you a calendar fridge magnet.

Your child comes home from school with new toys.

Where is the downside of receiving these things for free? After all, they're all generous acts.

If you accept free offers that'll genuinely add value to your life, then yes, these are kind acts.

However, suppose you're saying yes to things you know you don't need but are trying to justify them anyway. In that case, these offers are actually burdens.

Accepting free things for the 'potential' opportunity will likely result in more clutter, which means more decisions down the road.

Not only that, by continuing to say yes to various offers, you set the future expectation that you want more things that you don't need.

So here's the challenge. Default to no before you say yes. Start pushing back. Or at least give yourself some time to contemplate a free offer.

Sometimes receiving free things can't be avoided, and that's okay. You just want to get out of the habit of accepting anything and everything on the principle it was free.

8. Do the deathbed test

Not to get too dark, but if you were hypothetically on your deathbed today, and you were reflecting on your life, what would be your fondest memories? I'll wait for you as you write down at least three memories.

I bet your answers have little to do with the things you obtained and more to do with experiences you shared with others.

The quality of our lives is generally measured by moments of 'that was a good time', not 'that thing I had was awesome'.

So next time you find yourself longing to buy things to feel better, do the deathbed test to give you instant perspective.

9. Replace shopping with hobbies

According to data collected from the U.S. census, the average American over the age of 15 spends 10 hours a month shopping for consumer goods. While this number is gradually declining (allegedly from the efficiencies of the internet), it's still a significant amount of time to be spending on shopping activities.

I get it. Shopping often feels productive, fun and exhilarating. But what if we cut our time spent on shopping in half? We would free up an extra 5 hours a month to spend with family or even pursue the hobby or side-hustle you've wanted to start. This is not to mention the money you'll likely save.

To understand how much time you spend shopping, go back and review all of your consumer goods (not including groceries) you've purchased in the last month. Estimate how long it took to browse each purchase, including any online or offline research.

Do this exercise each month for the next 6 months. The action of tracking how much time you spend shopping will make it front of mind, and naturally, you'll start getting those hours back to do other things.

10. Treat your things like inventory

Once you've decluttered and Marie Kondo'd your home, you should have allocated space for everything you own.

The goal now is to treat your things like products on shelves in a store. Practically, this means is protecting the 'shelf space' for your stuff.

For example, before you decide to buy new shoes, look at your current storage situation for your shoes. Do you have a space on your shoe rack for a new pair? If not, you need to free up some space by getting rid of an existing pair before buying new ones.

The process of freeing up space for new items will add friction to acting on new purchases. It's no longer about exponentially adding things to your storage which you can't accommodate. You now have to be intentional about how many items you can hold at any given time.

I apply this principle to everything I own. I'm aware of how many free hangers are in my closet, how much space we have for cooking utensils, and how many shoes I have in rotation.

It's also common for parents to use the one in, one out method for managing their kid's toys.

Understanding your inventory makes your storage space more sacred. Therefore you'll be more intentional about what you bring into your home, knowing that you'll likely need to get rid of something else first.

11. Borrow or rent instead of buy

A simple method for getting your consumerism under control is to rent or borrow items instead of buying them.

Got a wedding or funeral to attend? Consider renting a dress or suit for the occasion.

Need to use a drill for building your deck? See if you can borrow one from your friends or family.

Running out of space on your bookshelf? Borrow books at your local library.

The added benefit of borrowing things is that it adds some time pressure to use them. Borrowing actually helps you overcome procrastination.

12. Turn your consumption habits into a game or challenge

If you're someone who likes a challenge, try a no-buy period – meaning, go without purchasing a non-essential consumer good for a defined time frame.

Get your best friend involved and see who can last the longest without buying anything. By gamifying our consumption habits, we turn what is perceived as restriction into empowerment and fun.

13. Practice minimalism

What's the ultimate alternative to consumerism? Minimalism.

A minimalist is someone who naturally rejects consumerism and sees value in having fewer things over more things.

Minimalism is a powerful philosophy that impacts how you view material things, your relationships, commitments, and digital inventory.

By adopting a minimalist mind-set, you give yourself a real chance of making sustainable positive changes to how you consume things.

How to avoid consumerism

Hopefully, after reading this guide, you have plenty of ideas to escape consumerism, create more time, save more money, and improve your mental health.

What about you? Do you have some of the symptoms of excessive consumerism? How have you overcome your habits?

16 May 2022

How does consumerism negatively impact our mental health?

By Emily Lidgard

Black Friday pulled at our purse strings this week, as it does every year on the 26th. With the alluring deals, many of us enjoyed a mini shopping spree this Friday. However, does this consumer mindset negatively impact our mental health?

The average modern-day consumer is subject to five thousand advertisements per day. That's thousands upon thousands of glossy, demanding messages imposed onto you from glimpses of eye-catching colourful billboards, to covert social media posts; we can scarcely escape them, from our own homes, to our phones. We are constantly surrounded by the message: 'SALE SALE SALE'

It is not only the advertisements to blame, but our own increasing need for new things. We accumulate and wish for an inexhaustible list of commodities. We are insatiable, constantly looking forward to the next new thing.

Why exactly do we enjoy shopping? We can look to our brains' responses to understand the essence of shopping's exhilaration. Even just considering purchasing a new item causes neurotransmitters to release feel-good chemicals like dopamine and endorphins, which become even stronger when we buy a new product. Though this effect sounds positive initially, you can actually become used to this effect. Resulting in a need to buy more and more things. It is no longer if you need the things you're buying, but an intense want for them instead.

The issues with consumerism aren't just limited to its physical effects but negatively harms our mental health through a number of other ways. A self-care boom swept the UK during lockdown, as it allowed us time to focus on ourselves. However, what started as a way to help mental health, may be beginning to hinder it. Self-care has been commercialised and bastardised by companies riding on this rising popularity. The market is so oversaturated, and it has become more about buying and trying the next new thing, then truly finding what works for you. Yet, the luxury moisturiser or sparkly bath bomb will always be ultimately unfulfilling, particularly without the mental determination.

Equally as detrimental as our compulsion to shop is the way in which we are convinced to shop. For women, in particular, the pressure to become the 'IT' girl is overwhelming. We are sold the cures to insecurities that the companies' manufacture.

These cycles and trends of fashion and innovation trap us in an endless cycle of wanting and buying and discarding. This is only becoming more insidious as marketers gain more information about you and advertisements become more targeted. Disturbing reports of advertisements targeting traumatic events range from women who have miscarried being shown pregnancy and baby-related content to those who suffer from eating disorders being shown dieting related content. Moreover, they actually target their advertisements to encourage self-consciousness. An internal report from Facebook disclosed that the company knows when its younger users are feeling emotions such as 'insecure', 'overwhelmed' and 'useless'. When considered with testaments from women who have been shown adverts to prevent menopause or fertility when they reach the relevant age, advertising seems to work to reinforce societal pressures when we are at our lowest.

So, how can I stop myself from participating in overconsumption and feel better about myself? While it may seem like a difficult task at first, one helpful method is to read up on movements such as zero waste and conscious consumption. It's useful to ask yourself questions about why you are buying something and how much you really want it. If you find yourself still yearning after reflecting on your purchasing habits, you could consider purchasing second-hand items to reduce the environmental impact. Although consumerism is commonplace and widespread, in doing as much as we can to limit overconsumption, we practise true self-care and look after our mental health.

29 November 2021

www.epigram.org.uk

Cost-of-living cutbacks: where are the public tightening their belts?

By Christien Phelby

In May 2022, global inflation hit its highest levels since 2008 – which has raised questions about how consumers can cope with the rising cost of living. While government intervention may make a difference in some markets, it's worth looking at where people are – and are not – likely to tighten their belts.

New YouGov data, focused on 17 different markets across Europe, APAC, the Americas, and MENA, indicates that three in five (61%) will be looking to reduce the amount they spend on eating out at restaurants first, saving money by preparing food at home. Half of the public (49%) also say they'd cut back on holidays and travel as a priority (49%); although with several markets reporting technical issues, queueing, and general chaos in international airports, saving money may not be the only motivation here.

Nearly as many plan to cut back on clothing (46%) first – which, with sustainability a significant concern in the fashion sector, may also be for reasons beyond simple cost-savings – and takeaways (44%).

Technology is another significant likely victim of inflation here: two in five (39%) say they are likely to prioritise cutting back on general tech purchases, with almost as many planning to limit their spending on video games (36%) or streaming services (35%) first. Leisure and entertainment may also take a hit: three in ten say they intend to spend less on sporting events (31%) or gambling (30%).

A minority are planning to reduce daily spending on expenses such as groceries (25%), automobiles (24%), and heating/lighting (23%) as a priority – in the latter case, markets such as the UK have seen prices of utility bills rise dramatically in recent months. A further fifth (19%) of global consumers will look to cut back on their mobile phone costs first.

The expenses consumers are least likely to attempt to reduce are insurance policies/premiums (12%) and healthcare costs (9%).

6 July 2022

Cost-of-living cutbacks: eating out and travel the first to go for global consumers

If your household budget is squeezed as a result of increases in the cost of living, in which areas would you first make cutbacks? Please select all that apply (%)

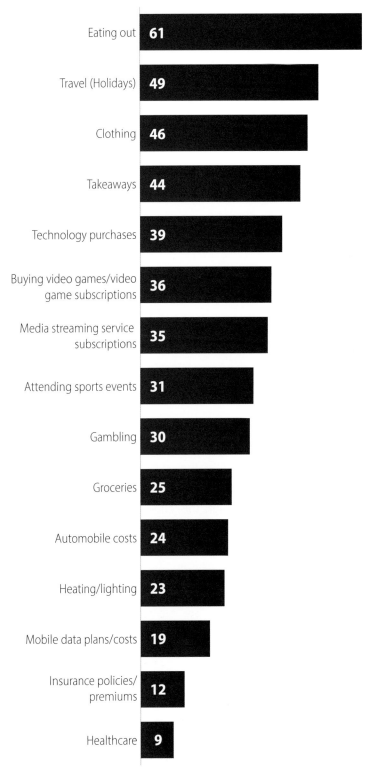

Eating out	61
Travel (Holidays)	49
Clothing	46
Takeaways	44
Technology purchases	39
Buying video games/video game subscriptions	36
Media streaming service subscriptions	35
Attending sports events	31
Gambling	30
Groceries	25
Automobile costs	24
Heating/lighting	23
Mobile data plans/costs	19
Insurance policies/premiums	12
Healthcare	9

Source: YouGov

What is fast fashion and why are clothing brands distancing themselves?

By Ciaran Clark

Fast Fashion is a dirty word in the clothing industry, rightly so with its devastating impact on the environment. But will our love for consumerism ever truly die out?

What is fast fashion?

Fast fashion is a term used in fashion retail for designs that are produced quickly to capitalise on current trends set by the big fashion houses.

It also applies to short ordering where it is made ready to go to market, with retailer orders being placed for the upcoming season rather than long ordering for the season ahead. This enables the clothing brand to be influenced by what is popular and selling at that time.

It's now developed a secondary meaning with the low production costs meaning it has limited wear before being consigned to the rubbish bin. The environmental impact of fast fashion has come under scrutiny, with consumerism highlighted as the main driver.

There has been an influx of fast fashion brands that have saturated the market with low-quality clothing designed to be sold via social media advertising and promoted by social influencers, brand ambassadors or through affiliate programs. This throw-away fashion is coming under fire with calls for sustainability in the clothing industry to be introduced, and most fast fashion brands now have a sustainable fashion range which some think is just greenwashing.

What is consumerism?

Consumerism is society's preoccupation with buying consumer goods, often influenced by advertising, social media or celebrity endorsement. It's the marketing idea that the consumer needs the products in their lives to improve their happiness.

In the ultimate consumerism, now you can get clothing delivered the same day as pushing a button on your keyboard, ready to wear for a night out.

What is the history of fast fashion?

The fashion industry accelerated in the swinging sixties with the increased demand for styles made popular on pop stars, models and actors/actresses on the wave of the sexual revolution and civil rights movement. The decade reacted to the dramatic changes in society with spontaneous fashion for mass appeal and would influence the future of womenswear by pushing boundaries now seen as the norm.

But in a consumerist sense, it was the new century that saw an increasing demand in the latest fashion at a bargain price. And as detailed in our history of streetwear article, the emergence of the internet opened up new levels of research and buying clothes. Prior to that, knock-off garments were often sold on market stalls and by dodgy-looking blokes in pubs. High-end names at high-street prices, a wardrobe staple highlighted by our spending habits on Black Friday. The ultimate in Champagne lifestyle on an Aldi Prosecco price tag.

The fashion houses knew people were happy to buy fakes with no regard for the fabric quality, so decided to improve their own manufacturing process for quicker turnarounds and lower price points. And it worked, the fashion industry was booming with its mass production straight to the willing and eager consumer.

These fast fashion companies are known as SPAs (speciality retailer of private label apparel) who manage the complete supply chain distribution channel, and everyone was winning. But the impacts on the environments came under the spotlight with the world focusing on climate change and cancel culture targeted fast fashion in their sights.

Couple that with the human rights working conditions and low minimum wage for garment workers, and the revolution for ethical fashion with low textile waste is on.

The impact of fast fashion on the environment

Due to humans' pesky need to breathe oxygen and the unfortunate bodily function of exhaling carbon dioxide, we all have a reliance on anything that does the reverse. As such, trees with their handy photosynthesis are literally a life-saver. And we need about 7-8 each to produce enough oxygen to breathe.

So it's no surprise that some people who plan to live on the planet in any sort of future, value oxygen and other life-critical things like food and water over clothes. Apparel factories produce roughly 10% of the greenhouse gas emissions, which contribute to global warming.

So why are clothing brands distancing themselves from being referred to as fast fashion?

Cancel culture and many articles on which fast fashion brands to avoid hits profits. And naturally, these companies have the mantra 'here for a good time and not a long time' and aim to make as much money as they can before they retire in the sunshine. In the ultimate fashion trend, they are now moving to sustainable fashion, promising they will do better in a bid to increase sales. In fairness, perhaps they do care about the environment, although there are many accusations of greenwashing.

So what is greenwashing?

Greenwashing is when a fashion brand spends more time and money on marketing themselves as sustainable or environmentally friendly, than on actually doing it. It's purely to give the impression to consumers to increase sales in that target demographic. The issue with this, is the clothes are still not made to last.

It's more commonplace with the oil companies of the '80s, while simultaneously polluting the earth with wilful abandonment. In short, labelling something as eco-friendly when it isn't, is greenwashing.

16 November 2021

How consumerism stole Valentine's Day

By Dr. Sophie King-Hill, Senior Fellow in the Health Services Management Centre (HSMC), University of Birmingham

Valentine's Day is upon us, and with it, many of us are buying gifts and cards for others to proclaim our love, care and affection for them. On face value, this seems like an innocent and pleasant thing to do. But once we start looking beneath the surface then the concept of Valentine's Day can appear more sinister.

Valentine's Day is a social construct. This means it doesn't exist outside of human perception. Now this doesn't mean that the roses, hearts, cards, gifts and gender-based advertisements are a figment of your imagination. What this means is that without the influence of human socialisation, the day is not an objective reality of its own.

The origins of Valentine's Day are somewhat hazy. With depictions of Cupid, the god of love from ancient mythology, often representing this day. There are also some links to martyred Christian saints named Valentine. It is also claimed that Valentine's Day is the hijacked pagan festival of Lupercalia, linked to fertility.

Whichever way we conceptualise the origins of Valentine's Day, it is not what it once was. It is no longer an innocent representation of caring for another but has become a capitalist venture aimed at consumerism.

This turn happened in 1913 when the first Valentines card was produced. From here, Valentine's Day consumerism spiralled into the heart-shaped, diamond-studded venture that we see today. For example, in 2009 the USA made £9.2 billion in revenue linked to Valentine's Day. This may be seen as a day to celebrate love, but when it is unpicked then the capitalist undertones are clear to see. In the current context of Covid where many people are struggling to make ends meet, then Valentine's Day can be viewed as an additional burden to an already stretched budget. And yet, people are concerned about missing out on Valentine's Day.

So why are we so conditioned not to question Valentine's Day and the stress and financial burden that it brings to so many? Well, it's useful to think about where it all starts.

From a young age, and by young I mean from early primary school, the conditioning begins. From age four, children in schools are drawing hearts and making cards for parents and carers for the 14th February. There are Valentine's Day discos and other events laden with heart-shaped cookies and gifts. So, instead of teaching our children to question and critically explore things that are foist upon them by a capitalist system, they are taught not to question and to 'buy in' and accept Valentine's Day as part of life.

Sadly, it is instilled in children that to show love and affection and to truly care for someone then you should buy something for them. This taps into our in-built need to be loved, wanted and accepted and that this love is attached to consumerist goods that need to be purchased. Children and young people are surrounded by Valentine's Day consumerism, from a very young age, via web-based ads, shop displays and the actions of adults. They aren't in a position to question Valentine's Day and it then becomes ingrained in them as a normal part of life.

But what message does this give to our children and young people? It tells them that love can be bought, that we have to spend money to show someone that we love them and implies that if they do not receive anything then they are less worthy. The financial cost of what a Valentine's gift has is now more central than the thought behind it, and this is rarely questioned.

Capitalism has weaponised love, one of our greatest needs, for financial gain under the guise of Valentine's Day.

14 February 2022

Halloween: a horror story of unnecessary consumerism?

And we thought the costumes were the scariest thing about Halloween! Dr Amy R Hackley, Senior Lecturer in Marketing in Birkbeck's Department of Management, explores the dark side of holiday consumerism.

As Halloween approaches, are you considering buying a pumpkin or two, and perhaps a plastic broom, make up or a horror mask for the kids to take trick or treating? Or even some Halloween-themed nightwear, or a special chocolate treat for yourself? Halloween consumption is on a rising trend: according to www.statistica.com, UK consumers are spending more than twice as much money on Halloween as we did in 2013, and an estimated 25% of us will buy a pumpkin, at a cost of around £30,000,000 (yes, that's £30 million). Total Halloween related spending is estimated at almost half a billion pounds sterling annually. Last year, British supermarket chain Waitrose reported its biggest ever Halloween sales bonanza, with sales up by 62% on the previous year. This year, in the home of Halloween consumption, the USA, pre-Halloween chocolate and confectionary sales have reached $324 million, up by 48% comparing to the same period in 2020, with American consumers spending a stunning $10 billion every year on Halloween. But why do we spend such extraordinary sums on trivial items to mark an ancient Celtic death festival?

Halloween originated as the pagan festival of Samhain, part of the ancient Celtic religion in Britain and other parts of Europe. The Celts believed that on the 31st October the barrier between the world of humans and the world of spirits dissolves to allow ghosts to wander amongst us on earth. The festival was needed to scare away the bad spirits, and to remember the dead. Turnips were used to carve lanterns rather than pumpkins, and 'guising' (going from house to house in masks and costumes) was practised. Under the influence of Christianity, the day became known as All Hallows' Eve or All Saints' Eve. There are versions of this festival practised around the world. For example, the Día de los Muertos or Day of the Dead in Mexico is celebrated in the 2017 Disney movie Coco, and across East Asia there are many versions of ghost festivals practised, such as paper burning rituals of ancestor worship, the Hungry Ghost festivals in Singapore and the 'Pee Ta Khon' festival in Dan-sai district, Loei province, Thailand. All these ritual practices are marked by consumption of various kinds, of food, goods and services. Halloween gained its popularity in America when 19th century Irish immigrants brought it with them, and the influence of American TV shows, books and movies, made Halloween more and more popular in the 20th Century.

From an academic perspective, consumption is a rich site of ritual practices, and death-related ritual is one of the most powerful. Death rituals re-enact our symbolic connection with our existence. They give us opportunities to re-tell stories about life and death, and to connect with the spirit world from which we are separated. They help the living to move away from the brute fact of death towards an acceptance of death as a kind of continuity of life. In a way, Halloween and other ritual practices help the living to celebrate life, by ritualising death.

Of course, the spiritual side of death rituals is very well-hidden in today's deeply commercialised consumer festival of Halloween. Although a lot of consumption is essential to the practice of death rituals, we really do not need to eat so much chocolate or to buy so many horror costumes. It is, really, a horror of wasteful consumption. Halloween costumes and decorations are made from cheap plastic and synthetic materials which are not so good for our environment. It was recorded that consumers created 2,000 tonnes of plastic waste by discarding Halloween costumes, and an estimated 8 million pumpkins (or 18,000 tonnes of edible pumpkin flesh) are heading for the bin as consumers do not eat it. But, when we are young, Halloween is an opportunity to party and have fun dressing up, trick or treating, eating a lot of chocolate and candy and, when we are older, perhaps drinking a lot of alcohol. What's not to love? Most supermarkets have their own dedicated range of branded Halloween products because the event is a huge opportunity to make money by selling us overpriced stuff we do not need.

Halloween remains one of the world's oldest holidays and death festivals, and in its many forms around the world it retains a rich cultural significance in human society. As the contemporary American author Andrew Delbanco notes in his book 'The death of Satan: how Americans have lost the sense of evil', he suggests that as we have lost touch with the idea of evil, we seem to need more vivid representations of it. The commercialisation of Halloween in the Western world helps us to affirm our sense of self and social identity and to reconcile us to the inevitability of death by making it seem like a harmless children's cartoon. Yet, lurking beneath the millions of pounds worth of fake blood, carved pumpkins and discarded plastic witch hats, is a real horror story of reckless and unsustainable consumption.

2021

Is Black Friday really worth it?

By Elizabeth Atkin

Today is Black Friday, a day typically full of mad dashes to secure top-notch deals and, in some cases, eye-watering discounts.

Been eyeing up a new 4k smart TV? A new coat? A new sofa or coffee table? Perhaps you're simply desperate to get your hands on some cut-price Christmas gifts and toys.

Whatever the case, it's important to make sure – before you hit Amazon or whack out the credit card – that the deal you're getting is really worth your cash.

And that you're not being swept up by the promise of major savings – especially if the item is something you didn't originally need to buy or even want.

To examine whether Black Friday sales are really worth it, Metro.co.uk has spoken to some of the UK's top analysts and consumer experts to dig deeper into the phenomenon.

Are Black Friday's deals all hype and no substance?

The expert opinion on Black Friday is mixed. Some say the deals are worth it, while others disagree.

Shorecap retail analyst Clive Black tells Metro.co.uk that the major shopping trend is, effectively, just a cash grab by retailers – and has been 'losing its lustre for a few years'.

He says: 'Shoppers should be very selective about where they spend their time online with respect to both Black Friday and Cyber Monday.

'Quite a few companies tried to sell consumers a whole load of stuff that was pre-meditated, or pre-bought specifically for Black Friday. As opposed to being a genuine sale.'

Clive notes that it's on the decline – with several major UK supermarkets 'barely participating' in recent Black Fridays.

He also says that, for 2021 in particular, there won't be a huge spread of deals at all – partly due to a serious lack of stock and shipping delays to Britain.

'An awful lot of product – that was due to be in store and in a warehouse before now in the UK – is somewhere sitting on the sea,' he explains.

'Indeed, it might be sitting in a Chinese warehouse or Chinese dock and not even on the sea. And so there is a material reduction in the amount of tat that retailers can flog to consumers this Black Friday.

'And so I think, in the main, it'll be a bit of a damp squib.'

Thinking about future Black Fridays, Clive predicts that – as the next few years pan out – the focus will shift to sustainability.

Something buying loads in the sales doesn't necessarily encourage, we must admit.

He explains: 'The days of fast fashion to the point of buying stuff and not wearing it again… I think those days are coming to an end.

'The sustainability agenda is starting to weave its way into people's minds: 'Do I really need that? Is this tat? Am I better taking someone out for a beer rather than buying [them] some tat?'

'This has been going on for three or four years now. But there's a changing attitude that values, relationships and experiences [matter] more than consumer goods.'

Ultimately, he reckons Black Friday's future isn't a bright one – but that us consumers will be the ones to make the final judgement call.

'I think [there will] be a gradual reduction in [the] potency [of Black Friday]… I don't see it being what it was five or six years ago. That massive, chaotic purchasing of stuff just for the sake of it.

'I sense more folks are starting to suss out what Black Friday has actually been about. And hence, the shopper will ultimately determine what Black Friday becomes.'

So when is Black Friday worth it, if ever?

Beyond hype and retailers trying to make a profit, surely there must be some benefit to the consumer?

Well, yes. But you'll need to be smart about it to make it really worth it, say the experts.

Retail analyst Clive does suggest that – if you're barmy for a specific brand – there's no harm in perusing their website to see what's on offer.

'I wouldn't say that shoppers should just ignore Black Friday,' he shares, 'But they should be prepared to be disappointed. And if they can [find] a bargain, then: OK, fair enough.

'Shoppers are savvy – and I think they've sussed that Black Friday is a lot of huff and puff and hype.

'In terms of what shoppers know they like, they should be alive to those brands throughout the year. You tend to find there are more frequent smaller sales now than big clearances.'

Meanwhile, Latest Deals (which has a dedicated Black Friday app) co-founder Tom Church reckons there is something left in Black Friday for shoppers.

Tom tells Metro.co.uk: 'Black Friday is typically where consumers go for technology, household appliances and furniture – and for good reason.

'These sectors are usually where the biggest discounts are applied, so it's a great time to pick up a new TV, set of headphones or sofa.'

But he does add: 'Shoppers should be aware that a number of issues are impacting the UK this year, such as fewer lorry drivers, massive order delays and shipping costs hitting the roof.

'This means that, when you do spot a bargain, it's worth grabbing it, as it will probably be in higher demand than usual.'

Ultimately: only you can decide if your potential Black Friday purchase is truly worth it. After all, it's your own money you'll be spending – nobody else's.

How to game Black Friday and ensure you get a good deal

There are a few ways to ensure you're getting the best deal this Black Friday.

But they all involve doing your homework, so you'll be paying not with cash but effort.

Hey, nothing good comes for free, right?

Make a strict budget

Firstly, decide in advance what you want or need to buy.

Don't let yourself get carried away with unnecessary purchases – unless, of course, you've got the cash to burn!

James Andrews, Senior Personal Finance Editor at money.co.uk, says: 'The key thing to do is to make sure you're actually getting a bargain – not just a hyped up price cut.

'If you are going to bag a bargain on Black Friday or Cyber Monday, don't go in blind. Start by making a wish list and noting what the current price is for the items on it.

'This will help you avoid buying things you don't need just because they're on offer. If you're planning to do Christmas shopping, your list should answer both who you'll buy for and what you plan to spend on each person.

'Once you have your wish list, you can set a budget. Black Friday isn't a day for browsing the shops and buying what strikes your fancy, it requires a strategic approach.

'If you come across something that's not on your list, only buy it if you're willing to cut something else from your budget.'

Think carefully about long-term value

If you're looking for an expensive piece of tech like a laptop, smartwatch, gaming system or TV, ensure you know which brand, model or what specifications you need.

And think carefully about what kind of warranty or repairs it may need, James warns.

'In terms of what items to buy on Black Friday weekend, history tells us that certain items get much steeper discounts than others,' he says.

'Large screen TVs can be a good purchase, but be warned, the steepest discounts are generally on mid-range TVs, rather than premium sets.

'Other good options include older generation tablets and laptops, although not usually Apple products, video game console bundles with extra additions such as games and controllers, smart home devices, headphones and home appliances.

'Another thing to be wary of when looking at Black Friday deals are the potential pitfalls that come with the purchase. Don't just look at the price of the item. There are useful extras that brands like John Lewis, AO and Argos offer that Amazon often don't.

'With items that you'll use for years at a time, such as household appliances like vacuum cleaners or kitchen sets – you'll want to pick up a long guarantee with your purchase.

'The cost of repairs to some appliances can be huge, so it can be well worth paying a little bit more elsewhere to save you money in the long run.'

Cross-check if it's really a bargain

OK, so you're in budget, sticking to your wishlist, and you're happy with what the item offers. What next?

Latest Deals' Tom says you need to check the size of the 'discount' against the RRP (Recommended Retail Price) – using a number of sources, not just the site you're buying off.

'As you browse through bargains, make sure the product you've got your eye on is a genuine bargain – it's worth checking the RRP to ensure it's a real deal.'

On Black Friday itself, start looking at different retailers to see what prices are being touted, too.

Keep in mind that Black Friday might not always offer the cheapest or most reasonable deal you can do.

Which? discovered some shocking information in a 2019 investigation: 85% of products advertised in Black Friday sales were cheaper at other times of the year.

Their research found that only 1% of 219 home or technology products advertised as 'Black Friday deals for 2019' had been at their lowest price on Black Friday itself.

The vast majority (85%) cost either the same price or less before and after the big sale day – with a whopping 98% actually cheaper to buy after Black Friday.

Don't let yourself fall for that hype. To check past prices on Amazon, use Camel Camel Camel to monitor when the item you want is usually at its cheapest.

Meanwhile, Price History is useful for Argos purchases – or do a wider search on various retailers using Price Spy or PriceRunner.

When it comes to the hundreds of Black Friday guides on the web, make sure you're reading a brand you trust to give you solid advice (like this one).

Don't get suckered in

And finally: if you're feeling iffy about a purchase, it's not the end of the world to click 'delete basket'.

Deals often continue throughout Black Friday weekend to Cyber Monday. And the January sales are just weeks away….

James says this could be the ticket to an even better bargain, adding: 'You can sometimes find better deals during end of season sales, Boxing Day sales or a couple of days before Christmas itself.

'Meanwhile, some retailers discount products in the days and weeks after Black Friday to get rid of stock left over from the big event.'

26 November 2021

Black Friday: The crux of consumerism

By Lucy Siers, Fourth Year Migration and Mobility

Black Friday is the pinnacle of reckless consumerism. It is a day constructed by brands to induce feelings of materialistic necessity to encourage hyper-spending through extreme discounts.

This day is a stark reminder of the ramifications that excessive materialism has on the rights of individuals at the bottom of the supply chain, weighed down by the greed of the Global North.

Black Friday originated from the US as a National holiday built solely to motivate shopping the day after Thanksgiving. This annual consumer shopping frenzy is generated via significant sales and discounts put on by nearly all major retailers.

Traditionally it was viewed as a day where customers would flock to their closest shops to make purchases. Some argue that, positively, this kept the high street alive. However, the transition of Black Friday purchases being made predominantly online has nulled this viewpoint.

Public awareness of the major social and environmental impacts generated by contemporary buying culture has risen. Through organisations such as Fashion Revolution, the importance of knowing where your clothing comes from has been thrown into the spotlight. Movements such as #WhoMadeMyClothes forces consumers to recognise their own complicity in this cycle of worker's rights abuse.

However, any progression made through these campaigns seems to be forgotten when Black Friday comes around.

In 2018, £1.49 billion was spent over Black Friday Weekend in the UK with the average UK shopper planning to spend £234 in total. These figures were even more shocking in the US, with American shoppers spending upwards of £6.46 billion on Cyber Monday alone making it the highest e-commerce sales day in American history.

The film The True Cost features scenes of frenzied American shoppers on Black Friday scrambling to grab all the goods they can carry. These images resemble apocalyptic-style mania. It is both saddening and angering to realise how hypnotised the public is by major discounts.

In 2018 *The Guardian* published an article that read, 'preparation is key' with all the major discounts to look out for and where to find the best bargain. Black Friday is portrayed as a race to accumulate the most goods at the cheapest price.

The Black Friday scramble taps into a major issue in the industry of careless overproduction.

The discount weekend is an excuse for brands to rid themselves of their stockpiles. I question how many of the goods sold over the weekend are actually masses of stockpiled items, or are in fact new and so demand an increase in production for that weekend.

Globalisation is the catalyst for this crisis development. With extensive trans-border trade and production leading to an internationally competitive environment that demands rapid production of quality products at low prices.

Global supply chains are a key component of this phenomenon. The composition of these chains enables multinational enterprises to attain cheap labour and resources regardless of geographical location.

Globalisation is the catalyst for this crisis

However, the rapid evolution of global supply chains meant that the countries targeted by multinational enterprises were not structurally or legally prepared to withstand the new influx of industry. These countries at the centre of the manufacturing stage of the chain have insufficient labour standards to protect vulnerable workers from exposure to corporate rights violations.

Black Friday exemplifies the production pressures that exacerbate these precarious working environments.

Vandana Shiva said that 'when we engage in consumption of production patterns which take more than we need, we are engaging in violence.' Consumer pressure leads to the evasion of national and international regulations so that products are manufactured as quickly and cheaply as possible.

Workers' rights have been rendered collateral damage of contemporary consumerist culture. The consumer and business mind-set has to be recalibrated to place the safety and well-being of the labour force as the central focus. By partaking in the Black Friday buying-frenzy, we are all complicit to the abuses existing deep in the supply chain.

Black Friday is symbolic of everything wrong with today's consumer culture and must be recognised as such.

29 November 2019

Psychologist explains how Primark customers end up buying things they often don't need

One tool is to increase 'dwell time' by keeping customers in the store for as long as possible.

By Jaymelouise Hudspith

I think everyone who has ever shopped at Primark has at one point or another walked out of the store with way more than they planned on buying. But according to an expert, it's not just a lack of self-control.

Stores including Primark use clever methods to tempt you into buying extra items, according to psychologists. This includes keeping you in the shop for as long as possible.

Psychologist Dr Amna Khan laid their discount stores' tools on the table during the Channel 5 documentary 'Primark: How Do They Do It?'.

In the documentary, she said: 'A destination store creates an experience for the consumer, almost like going to a theme park where all your senses are activated, and you want to stay there for longer.'

It is believed that Primark only buys large retail spaces and adds extra experiences like cafes and beauty services to tempt customers to stay in the store for longer, and thus, spend more.

According to the *Mirror*, consumer journalist Harry Wallop said: 'It's a phrase used in the retail industry "dwell time". You don't want people to just come in and buy an item and leave.

'You want someone to come in, look for the item, think "that looks like a nice cafe. I'll stop there, I'll then buy something else". On the way you spot another bit of homewares, it's only £5.

'If you can increase the dwell time you are onto a winning formula and you have justified the high expense of operating a high street store.'

Jermaine Lapwood, head of Primark's Innovation and Future trends, added: 'We want people to explore all the amazing products that we have to offer. But at the same time, we don't want them to be inconvenienced.

'If they want to get a coffee or if the kids are starting to get frustrated, they can pop up to our Disney cafe.'

And since the retailer doesn't sell online like many of its competitors, shoppers are forced to visit the store in person, where they're exposed to and tempted into buying more of its goods and services like manicures.

9 May 2022

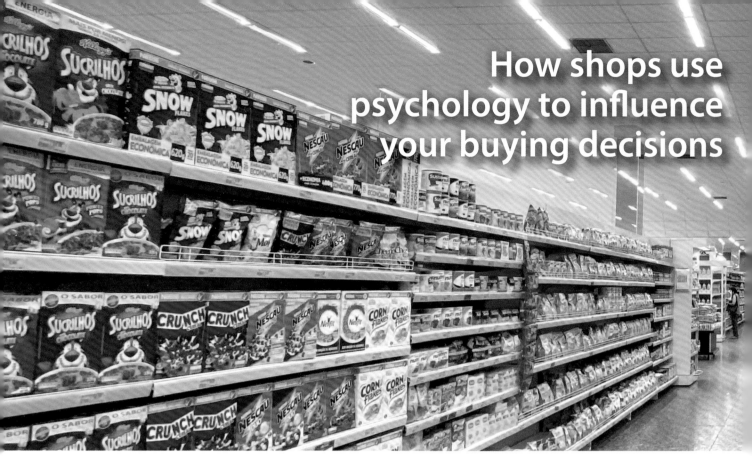

How shops use psychology to influence your buying decisions

An article from The Conversation.

THE CONVERSATION

By Cathrine Jansson-Boyd, Reader in Consumer Psychology, Anglia Ruskin University

You might think that you only buy what you need, when you need it. But whether you are shopping for food, clothes or gadgets, the retailers are using the power of psychological persuasion to influence your decisions – and help you part with your cash.

If you think back, I'll bet there's a good chance that you can remember walking into a grocery store only to find the layout of the shop has been changed. Perhaps the toilet paper was no longer where you expected it to be, or you struggled to find the tomato ketchup.

Why do shops like to move everything around? Well, it's actually a simple answer. Changing the location of items in a store means that we, the customers, are exposed to different items as we wander around searching for the things we need or want. This ploy can often significantly increase unplanned spending, as we add additional items to our baskets – often on impulse – while spending more time in the shop.

Buying on impulse

In fact, studies suggest that as much as 50% of all groceries are sold because of impulsiveness – and over 87% of shoppers make impulse buys.

While it is complicated and affected by many factors, such as a need for arousal and lack of self-control, it is known that external shopping cues – 'buy one get one free' offers, discounts and in-store promotional displays, for example – play a key role.

An appealing offer can lead to a rush of temporary delight, and this makes it harder to make a rational buying decision. We're overcome by the perceived value of the 'saving' if we buy the item in the here and now – so we ignore other considerations such as whether we really need it. The need for instant gratification can be hard to ignore.

Bundling is another technique that retailers use to trigger impulse buying.

You've probably seen it quite often. Complementary products are packaged together as one product, with one price, which often provides a substantial discount. Game consoles, for example, are often sold together with two or three games, and grocery stores have 'meal deal' bundles and even web pages dedicated to a whole range of bundle offers.

Shopping can be friend or foe

While these strategies can help to swell the profits of retailers, they can also contribute to problems for their customers.

Impulse buying can undoubtedly affect a consumer's mental wellbeing. It increases feelings of shame and guilt, which in turn can lead to anxiety, stress and depression.

And it's potentially even more serious when buying on impulse leads to excessive buying, especially if people spend money they don't have.

But there are some positives, too.

Online shopping has been found to give a dopamine boost, as it is released into our brains when we anticipate pleasure. So while we wait for our purchases to arrive, we tend to feel more excited than if we had bought things in store.

If this pleasurable feeling is well managed, then there's no harm in it. But, sadly, it doesn't always end there. That fleeting feeling of pleasure can sometimes lead to the onset of a shopping addiction. This can happen when a consumer wants to continuously experience the feel-good 'hit of dopamine', so they fall into a pattern of buying more and more items until it gets out of control.

On the flip side of the coin, shopping can help restore a person's sense of control.

When we're feeling unhappy or anxious, we tend to think that everything is out of our control. But as shopping allows us to make choices – which shop to go to or whether we like an item – it can bring back a feeling of personal control and reduce distress. So it can be a more meaningful activity than many think.

Retailers can help us too

While retailers might not be keen to reduce the amount of shopping we do, they could, if they wish, help to influence our buying decisions more positively.

There is a pressing need to combat obesity in most countries of the world. That's why the UK government has decided to restrict the promotions of unhealthy foods – those high in free sugars, salt and saturated fats – in prominent store locations from October 2022.

It's a strategy that could help.

Removing tempting treats from the checkouts can help to reduce the amount of sugary foods that are bought – in some cases by as much as 76%.

And a recent study found that by increasing the availability and promotions of healthier food options (such as stocking low-fat chips next to regular chips) – and making them more visible through positioning and clever use of signage – shoppers can indeed be encouraged to make better choices.

Ultimately, the key to resisting goods we don't want, or need – and making healthy decisions – lies with us. It helps to be conscious of what we are doing while shopping. A good personal strategy is to try to browse less and use a shopping list instead – and try to only buy what's on it. But be kind to yourself, because it can be easier said than done.

7 April 2022

9 dirty tricks supermarkets use to make you spend more money

Did you know supermarkets employ some cunning tactics to make you spend more money? Here's how they do it and how to avoid being duped.

By Ashleigh Mutton

So, you thought the supermarkets were on your side, helping you save extra pennies whenever they can?

While there are lots of great deals that genuinely could save you a packet, don't forget that supermarkets are out to make money from you, plain and simple.

From dodgy money-saving offers that don't actually save you money to multi-buys that cost the same as buying individual items, supermarkets use sneaky marketing tricks to get their hands on your hard-earned cash.

Arm yourself with the facts below and think twice before grabbing that special offer.

Sneaky supermarket marketing strategies

From a clever supermarket floorplan to not-so-affordable deals, here are the sneaky supermarket secrets they don't want you to know:

1. Floor layouts that make you spend more

It's crazy, but you wouldn't believe the amount of time and effort that goes into the supermarket layout – all with the intention of encouraging you to spend more cash.

Here are just a few of the ways they get you:

♦ Playing slow music to make you feel less rushed and happy to spend more time (and money) in store

♦ Putting healthy fruit and veg at the front so you shop there first and don't feel guilty about the less healthy foods that go into your basket later

♦ Placing essential items at the back and far away from each other so you have to look for them (and come across a few things you don't need but want to buy along the way)

♦ Keeping eggs in strange places so you end up on an egg hunt (and not the Easter kind)

♦ Stacking more expensive products at eye level and stocking popular combinations (like tortilla chips and salsa) next to each other to encourage you to get both

♦ Covering tills with last-minute 'essentials' to encourage impulse buying.

Some supermarkets have even been known to lay smaller floor tiles along the aisles that have more expensive stock, so the sound of your trolley wheels speeding up will encourage you to slow down and spend longer looking at the shelf items – mindblowing stuff, right?

2. Bogus BOGOF deals

The classic buy-one-get-one-free offer is a popular one. But while real BOGOF deals can be a steal, too often these offers are one of the many supermarket marketing tricks that don't work in your favour.

We've even seen situations where supermarkets have hiked the price of the item during the BOGOF deal, meaning it's actually cheaper to look for the same item not included in the promotion.

Take your time, look at individual prices and compare before you put something in your basket.

3. Multi-buy offers that won't help you save money

Some multi-buy offers (where you're told that you'll save by buying in bulk) can't be considered 'offers' at all.

While they won't cost you more, they often won't save you anything either, meaning you've just been tricked into buying way more of a product than you intended to.

For example, you might come across offers such as '3 for £3' when the item is individually priced at £1 each anyway.

This supermarket psychology tricks your brain into thinking you've got a good deal by getting more for your money, even if you don't need (or want) it.

4. 'Top deals' that aren't that top

When walking around your supermarket aisles, it's likely you'll be inundated with lots of brightly coloured signs for 'top deals', 'lowest prices ever' or other not-to-be-missed deals.

While these are supposedly products that have been reduced to a cheaper price than normal, we recommend having a good look at what the original price of the item was.

Research has found that many of these so-called 'deals' had been the same price for six months, while others had actually increased in price.

5. Leaving outdated promotions on display

A BBC investigation in 2017 found that Tesco had been particularly bad at keeping their displays up to date, leaving promotional branding up after deals have already ended.

The result of their experiment was that they were overcharged for their purchases at 33 out of 50 stores they visited. We're sure Tesco aren't the only offender, either.

Make sure you always check your promotion has been deducted at the check-out, and if not, show the display to a manager and ask customer services for your money back – that's your right as a customer. Some supermarkets will even pay you double the difference as a peace offering.

6. Misleading packaging

The fancy packaging of that 'high quality' bacon can convince you it's going to be much nicer, but will you really be able to taste the difference?

The packaging on supermarket premium brands is designed to tempt you into parting with those few extra pennies, but in reality, your extra cash is mostly just used to cover the cost of said fancy packaging.

Downshifting your weekly shop to value brands can save you up to £520 a year. Imagine what you could buy with that.

STS reader David Hamilton, from the University of Sunderland, also suggests staying clear of the 'to go' sections:

'Never buy food from the food-to-go section as they have the same food in much larger portions at a cheaper price in other areas of the supermarket. For example, pasta pots might be £2 for a small tub but in the main shop they'll have a pot double the size for £1, but maybe without a fork included.'

7. Encouraging shoppers to bulk buy

Thanks to wholesale supermarkets, it has been drilled into us that buying bulk-sized products over smaller items will automatically involve a saving.

Buying a massive tub of butter rather than a small one can seem like a good deal – by getting a larger amount in one go, you're saving on expensive packaging, right? But some supermarkets take advantage of that assumption and will price the larger tub higher than two smaller tubs which combined have the same weight.

They'll often also make it tricky to work out the weight-to-price ratio by labelling one product in grams and another in kilograms to throw you off.

8. Making comparisons impossible

This might totally go against your best instincts, but while packaged goods do normally cost more than loose items, this isn't always the case.

Supermarkets rely on the fact you think this way, and will often make comparing items confusing. This is particularly the case with fresh produce like fruit and veg. For example, packaged cucumbers will be priced per item, while the price for loose ones will be displayed in grams.

9. Online shopping substitutions

Unfortunately, supermarket tricks aren't just for in-store shopping. They also use them for your online food shop – nowhere is safe.

For example, you'll already be well acquainted with the sidebars they use to bring up similar items they think you might be tempted to part with more cash on, but you'll almost never see value brand items in there.

Also watch out for the 'allow substitutes' box – checking this means that they can change parts of your order if they've sold out, and replace it with something else.

Some people report being given more expensive items as replacements and only being charged for the cheaper version (neat!), but some have been known to throw in a more pricey replacement and charge you extra.

If you notice that something has been substituted when your delivery arrives, some supermarkets will let you refuse it at the door and have the driver return with it for a full refund.

The smartest move here would be to contact the supermarket customer service and find out what their policy on this is.

You don't have to treat food shopping like a SAS mission, of course, but by being savvy to these supermarket strategies you can watch out for duff deals and save yourself a few quid.

25 March 2022

Your favourite brands are scared of raising prices – but they'll sting you another way

You might find your box of Kleenex is missing a few tissues.

By Lauren Almeida

The spiralling cost of living crisis is affecting all aspects of British life, particularly at the supermarket. The average shopper will spend £380 more on groceries this year, according to the market research firm Kantar.

With inflation at a 40-year high of 9.1pc, it may come as a relief to shoppers to find that the prices of some of their favourite products have not changed.

But there is another way that brands are sneaking rising costs onto their customers – by simply reducing the size. This method of 'shrinkflation' has become increasingly common, as companies try to pass on the effects of supply chain disruptions and higher raw material costs – without the consumer noticing.

In the United States, consumers have reported that toilet rolls have shrunk, while ice cream – usually purchased by the gallon – has been melted down by several ounces.

In Britain, the food giant Nestlé cut the size of its Nescafé Azera tin of instant coffee 10pc to 90g this year, while the price remained at £5.49 in Tesco. A spokesman for the company said that this was because of higher costs in coffee beans, energy, packing and transportation.

Meanwhile, the maker of Cadbury Dairy Milk has reduced the sharing chocolate bar in size by a tenth to 180g, with the owner Mondelez International also citing 'significantly increased production costs'.

A spokesman for Nestlé said: 'We know that consumers face these higher costs too, and to avoid increasing recommended retail prices wherever possible, we do on occasions need to make minor adjustments to the weight of our products.' They added that final pricing was the discretion of individual retailers.

Other household goods have been hit by shrinkflation. A box of Kleenex tissues now contains 64 tissues per box, compared with 72 earlier this year, but costs the same.

A spokesman for the company attributed the reduction to rising energy, transportation and raw material costs.

Supermarkets are following suit. *The Telegraph* found that Tesco has reduced the size of its ready-made meals for one from 450g to 400g this year. A spokesman for the store did not comment.

The consumer group *Which?* also found that Walkers Classic Variety Crisps fell from 24 bags in a multipack to 22 bags in

Food inflation index

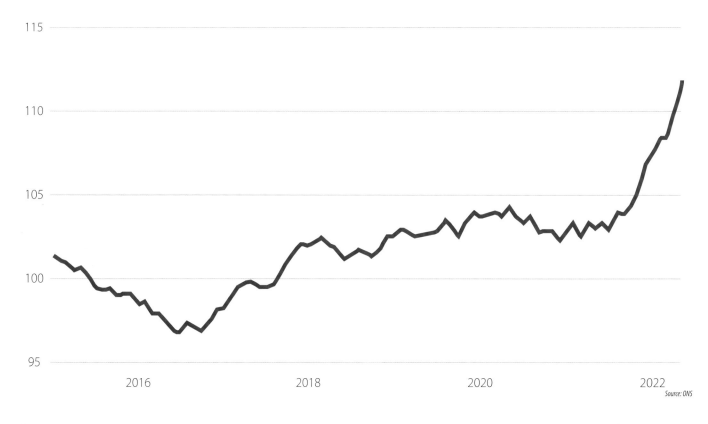

Source: ONS

Shrinkflation

Nescafe Coffee
10g lighter
Nestle has shrunk its Azera instant coffee tin

Kleenex
8 fewer
There are 64 tissues in the box, down from 72

Dairy Milk
10% smaller
Cadbury's reduced the size of its sharing bar earlier this year

some supermarkets last year, but have remained the same price. Walkers owner PepsiCo did not respond to requests for a comment.

Sue Davies, of *Which?*, said that this strategy of shrinkflation ultimately tricked shoppers into paying more for less.

'Supermarkets and manufacturers must be more upfront about the costs of their products and provide clear unit pricing so consumers can easily compare and choose the best value items,' she said.

'Shoppers are facing enough financial pressure from the rising cost of living without having to carefully check for changing packet sizes when they're doing the weekly shop.'

Despite rising costs, *Which?* also found that over the past two years, supermarkets have offered fewer discounts to their customers, and the availability of own-label budget ranges has reduced.

The number of promotional offers has fallen across all 20 of the most popular grocery categories, with bottled water deals falling the most, by 15pc, *Which?* added. That was followed by vegetables, where promotions have dropped 11pc.

Even the size of savings offered in promotions had fallen by three quarters on average, *Which?* found.

Rising food bills are adding further pressure on British households. Energy bills are now on track to pass £3,000 for the first time ever, according to predictions from the energy consultancy Cornwall Insight.

It forecast that the price cap on annual bills will hit £2,980 when it is next reset in October, before rising to £3,003.20 in January. This means that heating bills will have more than doubled in less than 18 months. The price cap stood at £1,278 in October 2021, before the outbreak of war in Ukraine sent gas prices soaring.

Households are also facing higher transport costs, with petrol prices reaching a new record high this week. The average cost of petrol rose to 189.33p a litre, pushing the cost of filling an average family car above £104, according to the RAC. Diesel climbed to 197.11p a litre, representing another new high.

23 June 2022

61% don't trust mega influencers to declare ads

New study shows perception gap in influencer compliance rates where 60.5% don't trust mega influencers to declare all ads despite just one complaint received for every 184.5k sponsored content pieces posted.

60.5% of UK don't trust that mega influencers declare all ads. 51.5% of UK don't trust that micro-influencers declare all ads. This is according to results from a new Google survey released today by social commerce firm, Emplifi.

Damning statistics capturing the breadth of a perception gap that doesn't match the compliance rate reality.

Last week The Advertising Standards Authority (ASA) and the Committees of Advertising Practice (CAP) published their Annual Report 2021. Complaints about influencer posts were shown to have increased by 20% to 4,889.

Whilst 4,889 complaints about influencer marketing content is too many, the number of complaints should be considered against content quantity. Conservative calculations show a minimum of 900 million pieces of sponsored content published each year by UK influencers on Instagram alone. That's one complaint for every 184.5k sponsored content pieces posted.

Why the perception gap? One possibility is that the ASA's newly-rolled-out influencer sanctions against repeat offenders are over-indexing in terms of publicity and impact.

Each Wednesday the ASA publishes a list of rulings it has made during the week. These may include influencer cases. Often the mainstream media picks up on these rulings especially where reality TV stars are involved.

The ASA has created an influencer 'wall of shame' or register held on its website of influencers who routinely fail to disclose advertising. This again is often picked up by mainstream media.

Most recently the ASA has started to take out advertising against persistent non-compliant influencers to make it clear that those influencers are not following the rules as the ASA described.

These new sanctions and the resulting negative publicity in mainstream media are helping the ASA attain their goals. According to their annual report 13 out of 17 persistently offending influencers came into compliance following the sanctions, including the first series of OPTA ads which ran in January 2022. Those who fail to comply will be subject to escalating sanctions.

Incidentally, TV was the second most complained about advertising media according to the ASA annual report. It made up close to half of all complaints (20,425). This despite TV ads being pre-cleared and television advertising being a well-established media channel - ITV launched in the UK 67 years ago in 1955.

2,503 UK consumers responded to a Google Survey in April 2022 commissioned by Emplifi.

24 May 2022

One in seven consumers in UK paying 'loyalty penalty', says charity

Citizens Advice says people should consider switching products such as mobile and broadband contracts or mortgages.

By Sarah Butler

About one in seven people could be paying a 'loyalty penalty' for products such as mortgages and mobile and broadband packages, according to Citizens Advice.

The charity said some UK households could save as much as £400 by switching, or seeking discounts, from their current suppliers.

Citizens Advice also said analysis of the budgets of 165,000 people who came to it for help with debts suggested people on lower incomes can end up spending nearly double the proportion of their income on telecoms that those earning more do.

Citizens Advice said it heard from a woman called Tracy who signed up to a £30-a-month package which included TV, landline, broadband and international calls in 2006. She relies on disability benefits.

In January this year, she started working through her bills to look for potential savings and was shocked to see her bill had increased to £80 a month over the years, the charity said. She has now switched providers.

She told the charity: 'Everything is going up: gas, electric, food, and I have a mortgage to pay. I shop late in the evenings to get yellow-sticker discounted food, I turned off my gas as I can't afford to repair the boiler or use the heating and I don't go anywhere other than my hospital appointments.

'When I asked my broadband provider why I wasn't told about the increases, they said I should have checked my payments and contacted them to see if there was a cheaper deal.'

The charity submitted a 'super-complaint' about loyalty penalties in the mobile, broadband, home insurance, mortgages and savings markets in 2018.

Measures to protect home and car insurance customers from loyalty penalties were introduced by the Financial Conduct Authority (FCA) in January this year. The changes mean insurers are required to offer renewing customers a price that is no higher than they would pay as a new customer.

Mike Emmett, who runs training for advisers at Citizens Advice Cardiff and Vale, said: 'Many people see their mobile and broadband as a lifeline. They need them to speak to people and do things like manage their universal credit account, and help their kids with their homework.

'But they're usually reluctant to switch for fear of rocking the boat, particularly because of the prospect of credit checks. We also find people who are digitally excluded or who have mental health problems often prefer to speak to someone about switching, but they can wait for hours on the phone and end up giving up.

'It's so frustrating when we see people who are on the lowest incomes paying the loyalty penalty, as they're forced to jump through so many hoops to try to sort it.'

1 August 2022

How the future of shopping was shaped by its past

An article from The Conversation.

By Rachel Bowlby, Professor of Comparative Literature, UCL

THE CONVERSATION

It's a sunny, spring Saturday morning in early 2019 and I'm having coffee at the local Costa in Brentwood, an Essex town where I've never been before. There are plenty of people out and about and smiling. I have a couple of hours to spare so I'm planning to wander around and have a look in the shops. Then my phone pings: 'Surprise!' It's a promotion from M&S. 'Here's 20% off when you shop online'.

The Brentwood branch of M&S is just a couple of doors down from where I am – I just passed it. But the notification isn't suggesting I go there. On the contrary, this special offer will deter me from shopping in an actual shop, on an actual high street, where I know I'd now be paying 25% more (if you start from the lower price) than I would if I bought online. It is, in effect, a counter-advertisement – taking me away from the shops and towards a virtual, online-only future.

Around this time, M&S had been closing stores in numerous locations. Many of these shops had been there for as long as people could remember, and were part of the towns' identity. Like 'our' NHS, and unlike most other commercial brands, M&S evokes a feeling of belonging to a shared history.

Looking back, my little counter-epiphany now seems to encapsulate something of the fraught shopping mood of three years ago. The incident felt like a painful sign of the contradictory state of British retail – and especially that part of it that is commonly known as the high street.

The choice on offer was absurd for both the customers (only one rational way to go), and the company (why push customers away from the stores that are still in use?). But it was somehow feasible then, in those innocent pre-pandemic times, to take for granted the inevitable triumph of online retail, even if it brought with it the destruction of most other modes of buying and selling.

From pedlars to supermarkets

Online shopping seemed in those days to be the next and natural step along the path that began with the introduction of self-service. I started charting these developments more than 20 years ago when I wrote *Carried Away: The Invention of Modern Shopping*. And a year after the sad Brentwood episode, at the start of 2020, I was coming to the end of writing my new book *Back to the Shops: The High Street in History and the Future*. This investigates the different stages of shopping, from its early beginnings to the present.

This history stretches back to pedlars and weekly markets and runs through small fixed shops in towns and villages to the grand 'destination' city department stores of the last part of the 19th century. Then, in the later 20th century, came self-service, to be followed in recent years by the move online.

But shopping history never moves in one single direction or all at once. There have always been regional and chronological divergences from mainstream developments. There are also retailing modes that fall by the wayside and then return at a later date in new guises or with new names. They often have every appearance of being newly invented.

Take fast fashion, for instance. We think of fast fashion as inseparable from a contemporary culture of rapid turnover. But a version of it can be found as far back as the 18th century, well before garments were mass-produced in factories. Clothes at this time were all sewn by hand.

In late 18th century London, a new type of shop appeared where, for a price, a lady or gentleman could commission a customised outfit that would be made up for them overnight. It offered an instant transformation into the style and class of the best social circles. But unlike modern fast fashion, it wasn't cheap and the clothes weren't flimsy or soon discarded.

The same period also saw the arrival of short-term shops not unlike those that we now call pop-ups. They might appear in any village, when an itinerant salesman rented a room in the local pub as a temporary location for what he'd present as a flash sale: 'now or never'. In the 1760s, for example, Thomas Turner, who kept the main shop in the small Sussex village of East Hoathly, complained in his diary about just such a character zooming into the area – and taking away attention, and trade, from his own steady service.

Today, pop-ups move into empty shop units on a short-term basis and at a lower-cost rental. It is a useful arrangement for both the owner of the premises and the shopkeeper. The landlord gets some (if not all) of their usual income for a space that would otherwise be yielding no income, while the tenant, with no long-term commitment, takes no great risk. The business itself – often selling time-limited, seasonal stock – is here today and gone soon after.

Mail order shopping also has a rich history that seems to anticipate later developments, too. Catalogue companies, like Freeman's or Kay's, were massively popular in the middle decades of the 20th century. But despite its popularity, 'the book' (the affectionate name for the big, 'full colour' catalogue) never posed a threat to the shops. Nevertheless, mail order was a form of virtual shopping at a distance, and now looks like a striking precursor to online shopping.

Perhaps the most surprising example of an early retail development whose beginnings have now disappeared from view, is the chain store. We tend to think of chain stores as having pushed independent shops out of the way in the late 20th century, with the result that every shopping mall and every high street (if it survives at all) looks like all the rest. But, in fact, chain stores were everywhere a century

earlier, including some of the names that are still well known today.

Chains took off in the second half of the 19th century. Nationwide grocery companies like Lipton's or Home & Colonial had thousands – yes, thousands – of branches by 1900. Of these early chains (or 'multiples' as they were then called) only the Co-op remains. The Co-op no longer maintains the cultural and trading pre-eminence it had from the mid-19th to the mid-20th century. But unlike the other dominant chains of that era, it has endured. It even pioneered the move to self-service in the middle of the 20th century and it remains a significant player among the biggest supermarket chains of today.

WHSmith, the newsagent and bookseller, developed from the late 1840s alongside the growing railway network. There was soon a stall to be seen inside every station of any size, providing the passenger with novels or newspapers for their journey. In 1900, there were no fewer than 800 branches nationwide. From the beginning of the 20th century, Smith's also had outlets on town shopping streets.

Boots the chemist was another 19th-century chain that is still a standard high street presence. The first Boots shop was opened in Nottingham in 1849. By the turn of the century, there were around 250 branches – and 1,000 by the early 1930s.

Numerous small and large chains, selling many types of commodity, faded away, died their deaths, or were taken over. But the striking point is that chain store Britain is nothing new. It dates back well over a century.

The self-service revolution

If online retail was the new feature of early 21st century shopping, self-service was the shopping revolution of the 20th century.

Self-service reached Europe after the Second World war. In the US, it had been an accidental invention of the Great Depression, when abandoned factories and warehouses were turned into makeshift, cut-price outlets. Customers picked out goods as they walked around and paid for everything at the end. By the 1940s, this new type of store was well established, often in regional chains, as the 'super market'. Postwar, this new American mode of retail operation was exported to the rest of the world.

Promoted as a modern, efficient way to shop, self-service entailed both a different type of store layout and new norms of customer and shopworker behaviour. Before this, every purchase made was asked for over the counter, item by item, and the assistant 'served' the customer personally. Few goods were packaged, so every order was literally customised: measured or weighed and then wrapped.

But self-service did away with all this. There was no need for counter service if customers were making their own selections. All available goods were put out on display, within reach. No need to ask someone to fetch them. And there was no one else waiting behind you for their turn to be served. You could take your time, look around – or get it done at speed. It was your choice.

This was a newly impersonal shopping environment. The customer was in control of the pace and the selection, but they were on their own and there was no longer someone standing there to serve them. For shop workers, meanwhile, the abolition of counter service meant that their various skills, including their people skills, were made redundant. So too was their often detailed knowledge of the products they sold.

When the customer did encounter a person across a counter, it was not to ask for advice about what to buy; it was simply to pay and get out. Now they just handed over a basket of goods already picked out; the assistant was not involved in the choosing. Nor was the checkout for chatting. Like factory workers, cashiers had to keep up to speed.

The whole process was meant to be more efficient, a saving of time and money for the benefit of business and customers alike. The customer, notably, was seen now as someone for whom time was a finite and valuable resource. In this way the shift to self-service was perfectly matched with some large social changes of the postwar decades.

As late as the 1960s, for example, 'housewife' was the default designation for women over the age of 16 (even though many had part- or full-time jobs). But the 'housewife' would soon be replaced by the double-shift working woman, eternally 'juggling' the demands of both home and work. By the end of the 20th century, now with the help of a fridge and a car, the daily walk to the local shops had been replaced by a weekly trip to the supermarket, where everything was available under one roof and the shopping was now a substantial task.

The first 1950s self-service stores are distant enough today to have become the subject of mild nostalgia, obscuring the original picture of smart efficiency. Black and white photos from the archives show people (particularly women) of every social type gamely learning to manage the curious 'basket' containers provided for them to carry around on their arms and fill up as they walked around the shop. These shoppers are no longer standing or sitting at the counter while they wait for their turn and that, at the outset, was the visible difference introduced by self-service. What looks odd now, many decades later, is how little they're buying – just a few jars and tins.

Save time online

With self-service firmly established to assist supposedly 'time-poor' consumers, the stage was set for internet shopping to promise an even more efficient way of doing things.

An Ocado flyer from early 2019 displays the caption: 'More time living, less time shopping', as if living and shopping have become mutually exclusive. And crucially, it is not money but time – its saving or gaining – which is the quantifiable currency of the promotion.

In this way, the online upgrade appears to remove all remaining real-life interference from the task of shopping. You don't have to take yourself anywhere to get to the store, which never closes. There are no empty shelves; everything is always there on the screen. There is still a trolley or basket, but not one that you have to push or carry, and it will hold whatever you 'add' to it, irrespective of volume or quantity.

The shop assistant is wholly absent from the screen, although there are downgraded virtual versions available in the form of programmed chat-bots. With online shopping, the backstage work that 'fulfils' an order occurs in a storage facility far away and is invisible to the customer. But in large self-service settings, like supermarkets and DIY mega-stores, the role of the checkout cashier had already been reduced to that single scanning function, requiring no specialist range of skills and no particular knowledge of any one of the thousands of possible things, from bananas to baby wipes, that they might be rapidly moving along.

Back to the 'real' shops?

Town centres had been dying a much discussed death for years, as more and more shops were being closed down – and stayed unused.

But amid the doom and gloom, some towns had been taking action to resist the trend, battling back with collective imagination and sometimes with significant financial backing. Shrewsbury Town Council revitalised a 1970s market building to make it a thriving centre for food stalls, cafés and specialist shops. The council also bought a couple of run-down indoor shopping centres in the town, which can now be redeveloped with community interests in mind.

On a smaller scale is Treorchy in South Wales, which won a national best high street prize in 2019 thanks to its flourishing independent shops and cafés. They all worked together to organise cultural events with the help of an enterprising chamber of commerce.

Still, initiatives like these were exceptional. For the places at the other extreme, where boarded-up units were everywhere, the call to keep shops open could sound like a hopeless plea, and too late to make a difference.

Lockdown's impact

In the first weeks of lockdown, it seemed that the pandemic would hasten the move online, by closing down most of the shops that were left – and seemingly leaving online as the only option. But as that slow, strange time went on, it became clear that something quite different was going on. Two years later, we can see that the lockdowns brought about a return to slower, more local and personal modes of shopping.

The shops still open for normal business – those that officially qualified as providers of 'essential' goods – were being used in new (and yet old) ways. They became places to go for some vital variation in our daily routines.

People also began to make a point of supporting and using independent, local shops. At the same time, home deliveries were being organised by these smaller shops, often working together in groups. This was the case with Heathfield, a few miles from Thomas Turner's village in East Sussex. And it was nothing to do with the networks set up by the supermarkets and other big chains.

In the media, shop assistants, working on checkouts or filling shelves, began to be referred to as 'frontline workers'. The implication of this 'promotion' was that they were doing invaluable work that was comparable to the public-spirited dedication of NHS employees.

The local high street seemed to be benefitting from renewed appreciation. It was as if the pandemic had demonstrated what shops were really for, and why we should not let them go. To say that shops – real shops – are a much needed community resource used to sound worthy and well-meaning. Now it just states the obvious.

A return to home delivery

Meanwhile, another, related revival is happening: home delivery. This is often assumed to have been an online invention, promoted by big supermarkets as the latest expansion of their networks and by big stores of all kinds. Some of the big home delivery names, such as Boohoo and Asos, have no physical shops at all.

But until the middle of the 20th century, most shops offered home delivery as a matter of course. For many food products, like milk or meat, this arrangement was the default. The butcher's boy brought round the tray of meat, and the milkman delivered the bottles direct to your doorstep every morning.

With self-service came the end of most home delivery services, too. When bigger supermarkets were built on the edges of towns, in the 1980s and 1990s, the basket became a big trolley, and people put all the bags they came out with into the back of a car. As with all the other changes associated with 'self'-service, the difference was that customers were doing this work themselves. The 'service' was no longer provided by others.

The new delivery services offered by smaller, independent stores that started up during lockdown represented a return to local arrangements of the kind that were standard before the arrival of self-service. Yet orders are often now made online. In this case, then, new technology has actively contributed to the revival of an older form of shopping.

In the East Sussex village of Rushlake Green, for example, the local shop began to offer home deliveries. This was so successful that they acquired a new delivery van with their name on the side. This marked something of a return to the 1930s, when local shops first started investing in a 'motor van' to make deliveries (a new trend much remarked on in the trade handbooks of the time).

As it happens, this joining of the traditional with the latest tech is itself a long established phenomenon in the history of retail distribution. New modes of transport and communication have repeatedly modified the existing conditions of shopping, and the current manifestation has striking antecedents.

Virginia Woolf's last novel, Between the Acts, offers a nice illustration of this. It is set at the end of the 1930s, when the installation of domestic telephones was beginning to make it possible for affluent customers to ring up the shop and order their meat or groceries for delivery, without having to leave the house or send a servant.

One scene in the novel has a country lady distractedly ordering fish 'in time for lunch', while she brushes her hair in front of the mirror and murmurs lines of poetry to herself. A few pages later, just as she requested, 'The fish had been delivered. Mitchell's boy, holding them in a crook of his arm, jumped off his motor bike.'

The narrator stays with this small domestic event for a moment, commenting on how the motorbike, a recent arrival on the local scene, is driving slow old habits out of use.

No feeding the pony with lumps of sugar at the kitchen door, nor time for gossip since his round had been increased.

In Woolf's time, this mode of transport, along with the phoned-in order, was a notable innovation, allowing just-in-time gourmet food deliveries. Almost a century later, the exclusive telephone is now the semi-universal smartphone, but the method of ordering at a distance is the same. And as it turns out, the motorbike has not been superseded in the online age of Deliveroo.

17 March 2022

Key Facts

- Every human being on earth is either a consumer or a customer. (page 1)

- Consumer rights are only given to consumers. (page 4)

- Your consumer rights are covered by the Consumer Rights Act 2015. (page 6)

- UK firms are spending a total of £9.24 billion every month to cover complaints handling. (page 10)

- 17.3% of UK customers are experiencing a product or service problem. (page 10)

- 33% of UK residents polled had left a negative review online. (page 11)

- In 2021 Ofcom received more than 145,000 complaints about broadcasts, a 400% increase on the previous year's figure of 34,545. (page 11)

- Consumerism is a social and economic order that encourages the acquisition of goods and services in ever-increasing amounts. (page 14)

- In May 2022, global inflation hit it's highest levels since 2008. (page 19)

- Half of the public (49%) say they'd cut back on holidays and travel. (page 19)

- A fifth (19%) of global consumers will look to cut back on their mobile phone costs. (page 19)

- The expenses consumers are least likely to attempt to reduce are insurance policies/premiums (12%) and healthcare costs (9%). (page 19)

- The first Valentines card was produced in 1913. (page 22)

- In 2009 the USA made £9.2 billion in revenue linked to Valentine's Day. (page 22)

- UK consumers are spending more than twice as much money on Halloween as we did in 2013, at a cost of around £30,000,000. (page 23)

- American consumers spend a stunning $10 billion every year on Halloween. (page 23)

- In 2018, £1.49 billion was spent over Black Friday Weekend in the UK with the average UK shopper planning to spend £234 in total. (page 26)

- In 2018, American shoppers spent upwards of £6.46 billion on Cyber Monday alone making it the highest e-commerce sales day in American history. (page 26)

- As much as 50% of all groceries are sold because of impulsiveness – and over 87% of shoppers make impulse buys. (page 28)

- Removing tempting treats from the checkouts can help to reduce the amount of sugary foods that are bought – in some cases by as much as 76%. (page 29)

- Downshifting your weekly shop to value brands can save you up to £520 a year. (page 31)

- Inflation is at a 40-year high of 9.1% (page 32)

- 60.5% of UK don't trust that mega influencers declare all ads. (page 34)

- 51.5% of UK don't trust that micro-influencers declare all ads. (page 34)

- About one in seven people could be paying a 'loyalty penalty' for products such as mortgages and mobile and broadband packages. (page 35)

Advertising

Advertising is communication between sellers and potential buyers. This can be delivered by various media, including radio, television, magazines, newspapers, billboards and website banners.

Black Friday

Originating from the US, Black Friday is a global shopping event that takes place the day after Thanksgiving. Retailers drop prices to mark the unofficial start of the Christmas shopping season.

Brand

A product or service distinguished from other products, usually marketed with a distinctive name, logo and reputation.

Capitalism

An economic system in which wealth generation is driven by privately-owned enterprises and individuals, rather than the state.

Circular economy

Keeping resources for as long as possible in order to extract maximum value from them, and then reusing or recycling the product (or materials from the product) instead of throwing it away.

Consumer

A consumer is anyone who purchases and uses goods and services.

Consumer rights

A consumer has the right to expect certain standards in the goods they buy. The law says that the goods must be of satisfactory quality, fit for their purpose and as described. These statutory rights cover all goods bought or hired from a trader, including goods bought in sales.

Credit

A consumer can obtain goods and services before payment, based on an agreement that payment will be made at some point in the future. Other conditions may also be imposed. Forms of credit can include personal loans, overdrafts, credit cards, store cards, interest-free credit and hire purchase. However, reliance on credit can result in high levels of consumer debt.

E-commerce

Electronic business transactions, usually occurring via the Internet, e.g. purchasing goods online.

E-tail

A play on the word `retail`, this refers to shopping online.

Economy

The way in which a region manages its resources. References to the `national economy` indicate the financial situation of a country: how wealthy or prosperous it is.

Ethical consumerism

Buying things that are produced ethically – typically, things which do not involve harm to or exploitation of humans, animals or the environment; and also by refusing to buy products or services not made under these principles.

Expenditure

The act of paying out money.

Fast fashion

Inexpensive, mass-produced clothing that is usually produced quickly to respond to current fashion trends. Often, it is only worn a few times before being thrown away.

Ofcom

The independent regulator for all radio, television and telecom broadcasting in the UK. Ofcom deal with all consumer complaints regarding television or radio, issue broadcasting licences and promote competition. Ofcom are Government-approved and act under the Communications Act 2003.

Recession

A period during which economic activity has slowed, causing a reduction in Gross Domestic Product (GDP), employment, household incomes and business profits. If GDP shows a reduction over at least six months, a country is then said to be in recession. Recessions are caused by people spending less, businesses making less and banks being more reluctant to give people loans.

Scam

A scam is a scheme designed to trick consumers out of their money. Scams can take many forms, and are increasingly perpetrated over the Internet: 'phishing' scams, where a web user is sent an email claiming to be from their bank in order to gain access to their account, is one common example.

Shrinkflation

The process by which a product's size is reduced while its price remains the same. Meaning consumers are paying more for less.

Sustainability

Sustainability means living within the limits of the planet's resources to meet humanity's present-day needs without compromising those of future generations. Sustainable living should maintain a balanced and healthy environment.

Throwaway/throw-away society

A society where rather than re-using or recycling something, people just throw it away. This is strongly influenced by consumerism, the increased consumption of goods.

Activities

Brainstorming

- In small groups, discuss what you know about consumerism. Consider the following points:
  - What is consumerism?
  - What is a 'brand'?
  - What do we mean by 'ethical consumerism'?
  - What does the term 'materialistic' mean and how does this relate to consumerism?
  - What are consumer rights?

- In pairs, discuss the difference between a customer and a consumer.

Research

- Conduct some research amongst your friends and family to find out what matters to them most when making a purchasing decision: brand, price, quality, company ethics? Write a report to analyse your findings and include a graph or infographic.

- Conduct a questionnaire amongst your class to find out how much people spend when they go shopping. You should compare and contrast the differences between males and females, and ask people about their online shopping habits as well as when they physically visit the shops. Write a report to analyse your findings and include a graph or infographic.

- Visit your local high street and count the number of shops that are vacant or closing down. Feedback to your class and discuss why you think high streets are changing.

- Choose a brand that you are familiar with and research the techniques they use to encourage people to buy their products/services. For example, advertising campaigns, tie-ins with films or TV sponsorship, etc. Write a short paragraph summarising your findings.

Design

- Design a poster that will encourage people to make ethical purchasing decisions.

- Choose one of the articles in this book and create an illustration to highlight the key themes/message of your chosen article.

- Design your own product – it could be trainers, perfume or a soft drink, for example. Individually or in groups, create a 'brand' around your new product including a name, logo and slogan. Think about who your product is aimed at and how you would reach that target audience.

- Using the article 'How to avoid the trap of consumerism', design a poster to highlight some key points.

- Design a poster to highlight consumer rights.

Oral

- In groups, discuss how social media puts pressure on people to consume the 'right' brands. How important is it to acquire the 'right' brands and why are they associated with achieving happiness?

- In pairs, role-play a situation in which one of you is trying to convince the other to boycott a particular product or company. Think carefully about what you will say to persuade your partner and validate your argument.

- Ask a relative who is older than you how they think consumerism has changed in the last ten years. Write some notes and feedback to your class.

- In small groups, discuss the future of shopping. How do you think things may change over the next 50 years?

- As a class, discuss what you think about 'influencer' marketing. Do you think that it is always easy to tell if an influencer is advertising a product or not?

Reading/writing

- Write a blog post about the rise of mindful consumerism. Have you noticed your own consumer behaviour changing recently – if so, give some examples.

- Imagine you work for a charity that promotes ethical consumerism. Plan a social media campaign that will encourage people to change their shopping habits.

- Have a look at a newspaper. How many adverts can you see? Write a paragraph on the different types of adverts. Consider who they are aimed at and what products they are for.

- Choose one of the articles in this book and write a one-paragraph summary. Pick three key points from the article.

Acknowledgements

The publisher is grateful for permission to reproduce the material in this book. While every care has been taken to trace and acknowledge copyright, the publisher tenders its apology for any accidental infringement or where copyright has proved untraceable. The publisher would be pleased to come to a suitable arrangement in any such case with the rightful owner.

The material reproduced in **issues** books is provided as an educational resource only. The views, opinions and information contained within reprinted material in **issues** books do not necessarily represent those of Independence Educational Publishers and its employees.

Images

Cover image courtesy of iStock. All other images courtesy of Freepik, Pixabay and Unsplash.

Additional acknowledgements

With thanks to the Independence team: Shelley Baldry, Tracy Biram, Klaudia Sommer and Jackie Staines.

Danielle Lobban

Cambridge, September 2022